Cambridge E

Elements in Public Policy
edited by
M. Ramesh
National University of Singapore
Michael Howlett
Simon Fraser University, British Colombia
Xun Wu
Hong Kong University of Science and Technology
Judith Clifton
University of Cantabria
Eduardo Araral
National University of Singapore

DEFINING POLICY ANALYSIS: A JOURNEY THAT NEVER ENDS

Beryl A. Radin

CAMBRIDGE
UNIVERSITY PRESS

CAMBRIDGE
UNIVERSITY PRESS

University Printing House, Cambridge CB2 8BS, United Kingdom

One Liberty Plaza, 20th Floor, New York, NY 10006, USA

477 Williamstown Road, Port Melbourne, VIC 3207, Australia

314–321, 3rd Floor, Plot 3, Splendor Forum, Jasola District Centre,
New Delhi – 110025, India

79 Anson Road, #06–04/06, Singapore 079906

Cambridge University Press is part of the University of Cambridge.

It furthers the University's mission by disseminating knowledge in the pursuit of
education, learning, and research at the highest international levels of excellence.

www.cambridge.org
Information on this title: www.cambridge.org/9781108927802
DOI: 10.1017/9781108933193

© Beryl A. Radin 2020

First published 2020

A catalogue record for this publication is available from the British Library.

ISBN 978-1-108-92780-2 Paperback
ISSN 2398-4058 (online)
ISSN 2514-3565 (print)

Defining Policy Analysis: A Journey that Never Ends

Elements in Public Policy

DOI: 10.1017/9781108933193
First published online: December 2020

Beryl A. Radin

Author for correspondence: Beryl A. Radin, berylradin@verizon.net

Abstract: For much of its life, the field of policy analysis has lived with a wide range of definitions of its goals, work, and significance in the society. This Element seeks to sort out these differences by describing the issues, players, and developments that have played a role over the life of this field. As a result of the relationships that have developed, an environment has emerged where both academics and practitioners who self-identify as "policy analysts" are not always recognized as such by others who use that same label.

This Element explores the reasons why this conflictual situation has developed and whether the current status is a major departure from the past. While these developments may not be new or found only in policy analysis, they do have an impact on the status of the academics as well as the practitioners in the field.

Keywords: advising, analysis, policy, clients, conflict, practitioners

ISBNs: 9781108927802 (PB), 9781108933193 (OC)
ISSNs: 2398-4058 (online), 2514-3565 (print)

Contents

1 Introduction: Searching for an Identity

For much of its life, the field of policy analysis has lived with a wide range of definitions of its goals, work, and significance in the society. Conversations between people who self-identify as policy analysts sometimes seem to be straight from the Tower of Babel, where individuals speak different languages and have difficulty communicating with one another. This Element seeks to sort out these differences by describing the issues, players, and developments that have played a role across the life of this field. It is my hope that readers will find a picture of themselves in this discussion.

I signed my agreement with Cambridge University Press for a manuscript as part of their Academic Elements offerings just as the Coronavirus began to creep into my consciousness. As a result, the process of writing this manuscript was entwined with one of the most unsettling experiences of my life. Not only was my life disrupted by a day-to-day, hour-by-hour schedule that seemed to parallel experiences of wartime, it was also a direct challenge and attack on my personal values and beliefs.

Given my age, I had envisioned this Element as the last volume that I would write. I was motivated to write it because, right before my eyes, I was watching the metamorphosis of one of my major areas of professional interest move into very different forms. Even before COVID-19 emerged, I saw the field of policy analysis change dramatically. While I hadn't connected the two developments before I sat down in front of my computer, writing this manuscript has inevitably linked the two.

This is not surprising. My personal, professional, and value concerns have always moved in the same direction and, as a result, have affected one another. I tend to see how decisions made about one set of concerns interplays with another set of concerns and, hence, have personalized what for some move along separate tracks. I have made decisions about where to live, where to enroll in educational programs, what jobs to take, what to study, and where to spend time on volunteer activities in a way that links what others may see as separate moves.

Much of my previous published work has focused on the historical developments in the policy analysis field – the developments that I have seen from both inside and outside perspectives. Citizenship and public policy issues have been a part of my entire life. Originally trained as an historian, I have always been sensitive to the shifts in the intellectual history that surrounds the policy analysis field. I've usually emphasized the changes that emerged from incrementalism, but in recent years I have tended to become more skeptical about the extent of change that is possible in the twenty-first century and the ways that seemingly diverse issues affect one another.

Over the years, I have noted the changes that have occurred in the field from several perches. One emerged from nearly fifty years of teaching graduate students in policy analysis. The second came from my own involvement in the policy world, either as an analyst, an advocate, or an interested citizen. I've been quite aware of the generational changes that have occurred, especially in the current generation of students, who seem to anticipate a conflict between the jobs available to them and their personal values.

Increasingly, I have become more concerned about the directions taken in the journey that something titled "policy analysis" was taking. As the years progressed, I found myself attending familiar conferences but, despite my presence, failing to find many sessions on the program that seemed to be important or even interesting to me. These were often conferences sponsored by groups in which I had played a leadership role. One could link this perception to my advanced age and the changes that are easily ascribed to it, but I had an underlying hunch that it reflected something more substantive.

This Element is my attempt to give readers a sense of my exploration of this issue. I begin by acknowledging that there are few fields in the social sciences that have ignored the multiple effects of economic, social, and political change. Thus, one should not be surprised by shifts in the way the field is defined and organized. Most of the disciplines have managed to balance these demands with classic issues and create variations on familiar themes. These changes were often built into standard operating procedures and were not always immediately visible. While modifying the past assumptions and approaches associated with the relevant social science discipline, these fields still contain issues, methodologies, and processes that resonate with those of the past.

While changes in the original assumptions seemed obvious and appropriate, there has been a pattern of variations on the original assumptions that often seemed familiar. Over the years, issues have appeared on agendas that never seem to have been resolved or even formally acknowledged. This is especially true for policy analysis.

As a result of the relationships that have developed over the years, an environment has emerged where both academics and practitioners who self-identify as "policy analysts" are not always recognized as such by others who use that same label. Some who have been regular attendees at organizations such as APPAM (the United States-based Association of Public Policy Analysis and Management) find that they are uncomfortable participating in the recent discussions that have taken place in those settings. Others have the opposite reaction and do not acknowledge the potential import of the past patterns. Neither group recognizes the other group's players, issues, and approaches, and they certainly don't agree about their relative importance. While this may be most visible in the US organizations, there are traces of similar reactions in other parts of the globe.

This Element attempts to explore the reasons why this conflictual situation has developed and whether the current status is a major departure from the past. While these developments may not be new or found only in policy analysis, they do have an impact on the status of the academics as well as the practitioners in the field. Both the form and the impact of these activities appear to have diminished the ability of policy analysts to improve the societies in which they live. This is ironic since that was the basic goal of those who saw themselves as the original policy analysts. This exploration of the policy analyst's role draws on a range of sources to illustrate my argument; these include activities and writings of a number of individuals identified with changes in the field, and draw on both writings and activities over time.

My approach is historical in nature, but I am trying to define the nature of the current state of the field by placing it in the context of past developments. I believe that the topic that most interests policy analysts today seems to begin with concern about whether data is available. Is that concern inevitable, and does its ascendant role lead one to address a policy problem and lead to change?

Collectively, we seem to have forgotten that this field started in the world of practice and then moved to the academy. Both sites care about data, but their definition of data differs. For some, the data becomes an end in itself and not a means to other ends. Yet today it seems that we as a collectivity are largely uninterested in developments in the world of practice.

I have focused this discussion on a number of different topics that seem to me to tell the story of how these changes have led to these developments. Each of the topics will be discussed separately but will highlight the changes that have taken place, the players in these modifications, their contributions, and the impact of these changes on the field. The concluding section will attempt to provide readers with a way to assess their personal pattern and craft future directions for themselves.

This perspective is not completely sui generis. There are some people in the field who seem to share my views. I have discovered some people with similar perceptions. Interestingly enough, almost all of them had some link to the public policy efforts found at the University of California at Berkeley in the period from the late 1960s to the 1980s. The activities that were led by Aaron Wildavsky during this period were significant in the creation of the policy analysis field. This occurred through the development of both the MPP (Masters of Public Policy) and the PhD in public policy at Berkeley, as well as the development of journals and the field in general

Wildavsky's role in defining and developing a unique academic program has rarely been acknowledged by later generations of policy analysts, either in the US or in other countries as the field expanded across the globe. Yet, if one imposed a family tree framework on the several generations of policy analysts who emerged throughout the last third of the twentieth century, something that touched the Berkeley school appeared in the background of many of the significant players. They are not always labeled as policy analysts, but emerge in different places and at different times.[1]

This short volume is not a traditional work. It does not fit the model of any earlier publication I know of. In some respects it is a memoir, since I was a witness to a number of the developments that I describe. But I was on the periphery of many of the changes that took place in Washington, in Berkeley, and in the United States more generally. More recently, I have been involved in efforts in a number of countries (largely in Asia) and have observed comparative developments there. I am not arguing that the field is moving in clear directions. In fact, as time has progressed the field has become more complex and often conflictual.

But this Element does have several goals. First, it is meant to be a tribute to Wildavsky, whose creativity and ability to predict issues that would play a role in the future development of the field is currently underappreciated and frequently ignored. In some ways, one feels that Wildavsky left us in the middle of a conversation. Second, it seeks to provide readers with an understanding of the dynamics and issues that seemed to be the basis for the situation I describe. Like many policy areas themselves, the issues have taken on the complexity of the twenty-first century. As I have noted, many of those who call themselves "policy analysts" define themselves in totally different ways than those who emerged from the early years. Not only have these definitions led to different emphases and approaches, but they often generate conflict between proponents who do not accept the definitions of others who explain the origins, meanings, and requirements of the field very differently. And third (and perhaps most importantly), it is a picture of what some call "the best laid plans," as it tells the story of the development of the field as it has responded to uncertainty and change. Readers are likely to find that they cannot find their favorite author or example from all three areas in the volume. Hopefully, however, this Element will be interesting to its readers, particularly those entering the policy analysis field. `

---

[1] Among the individuals who were at Berkeley during the early period of the School, either as faculty or as students in the School (or in related programs), were Eugene Bardach, Arnold Meltsner, David Weimer, Aidan Vining, Helen Ingram, Jeanne Nienaber Clark, Howell Baum, Iris Geva May, Eric Patashnik, David Dery and Frank Thompson.

1.1 Are the Developments in Policy Analysis Different from Those in Other Social Sciences?

One should not be surprised that a field such as policy analysis has changed since the 1960s. There are few fields in the social sciences that have ignored the multiple effects of economic, social, and political change. Most of the disciplines (e.g. political science, sociology, planning, economics, and others) have managed to turn these demands into classic issues and create variations on familiar themes.

But this is not the case for the policy analysis field. While the roles and functions of policy advising are ancient, policy analysis as a modern academic and practice field is really quite new (see Goldhamer, 1978). Despite the attention given to it, policy analysis as an identifiable academic and practitioner area is less than sixty years old. It started as a self-conscious field of practice in the United States in the 1960s, moved into an academic setting in the form of degree programs largely in the United States, and by the twenty-first century responded to international and global interest.

While changes in the original assumptions often seemed obvious, there has been a pattern of variations on those original assumptions that are more puzzling. At times it seems to operate as an octopus with tentacles reaching into many other subject areas. The boundaries between these elements are confusing and sometimes exhibit intellectual variations of imperialism or attention to limited issues that have emerged as a result of somewhat idiosyncratic developments. It is not always clear whether policy analysis is overtaken by other agendas and approaches or whether it plays the ascent role.

These changes have produced a contemporary field and a definition of "policy" that is a strange combination of wide breadth and narrow depth of issues. Members of the International Political Science Association recognized these relationships by spinning off a number of its substantive sections to a freestanding organization and created the International Public Policy Association. Yet it is not always clear what should be included under that banner, and the emphasis on the inheritance from the political science field does not always clarify the boundaries of the policy analysis term.

As a result of these complex relationships, an environment has emerged where both academics and practitioners who self-identify as "policy analysts" are not recognized as such by others who use that same label. Some who have been regular attendees at organizations such as APPAM find that they are uncomfortable participating in the recent discussions that have taken place in those conferences and settings. Others have the opposite reaction and do not acknowledge the potential import of the past patterns. Neither group recognizes the issues and approaches emphasized by other groups – and they certainly don't agree about their relative importance.

2 Section One: The Origins of the Policy Analyst Concept and its Early History

This Element attempts to explore the reasons why this complex situation has developed. Why is there so little agreement on what a policy analyst is and should do? While these developments may not be new or found only in policy analysis, they do have an impact on the status of the academics as well as the practitioners in the field. And it is not surprising that many of these efforts have had limited ability to improve the societies in which we live – the basic goal of those who saw themselves as the original policy analysts. Despite its expectations and promises, the search for a definition of the policy field has become a quest that seems to be present throughout the life of the policy analysis field. I will draw on a range of sources to illustrate my arguments. These include the activities and writings of a number of individuals identified with changes in the field, and their writings and activities are analyzed over time.

2.1 The Origins of the Policy Analysis Concept

The term "policy analyst" did not really appear in the literature until early in the 1960s. It emerged from the post–World War II experience that produced the RAND Corporation and the use of intellectual approaches that drew on the systems analysis field.[2]

This story begins with a discussion of the efforts in the US Department of Defense and related activities in other parts of the US Federal Government during the 1960s. This draws on the work of RAND staff member Herbert Goldhamer who, by the late 1970s, found enough in the literature and practice to publish a book that opened with the following introduction:

> The advisers to political leaders do not lack for attention in contemporary political journalism, in political biography, and in memoirs. In addition, a substantial literature now exists on the role of the expert and adviser in government service in the United States and Great Britain during and after World War II. Oddly enough, however, there is, to my knowledge, no work on the adviser that covers a sufficient range of periods and cultures to throw into relief the continuities and diversities of this political figure over the centuries in which he has played his important role in politics. (Goldhamer, 1978, p. ix)

---

[2] RAND is a non-profit organization created in 1948, just after World War II, to do analytic work for the US government, especially the Department of Defense. It was designed to further and promote scientific, educational, and charitable purposes for the public welfare of the United States.

Goldhamer's goal in the volume was to describe a range of advisers drawn from a variety of eras and cultures that would illustrate the "continuities and diversities of this political figure" over four millennia (Goldhamer, p. 3). He notes that "The political adviser appears in man's earliest surviving documents and has never disappeared from the political stage since that time." While popular culture sometimes defines Machiavelli as the original policy analyst, Goldhamer's definition emphasizes elements that move beyond a focus on the power relationship between a decision-maker and someone who advised that person.

Goldhamer's unusual book focused on individuals who met the following criteria:

• They were advisers to the supreme leader of a nation;
• They came from diverse elements in the society but from established professions;
• They were almost always men;
• Occasionally they were "wandering scholars" who did not see their role as long-term players;
• They had access to the leaders;
• They believed that the timing of action was important;
• They had an "analytical mind" that drew on "calculation, rationality, efficiency, planning, and theory" but also had an "intuitive mind";
• Their expertise derived from practice, experience, or experiment (Goldhamer, 1978, chapter 5).

For Goldhamer, the last criterion often linked the adviser to the role of a manager. As such, it became a part of the British civil service system that developed within the Westminster political system and the British Empire. Top-level bureaucrats in that system were expected to operate as advisers to the top officials in the bureaucracy and are likely to have advised ministers on issues and practices that they themselves eventually implemented. But they did not tend to use the term "policy analyst" to describe themselves. Instead, as one British academic put it, the "bias towards prescriptive analysis – towards the analysis of the 'improvement' of policy processes and policies themselves – certainly influences the policy approach" (Hogwood and Gunn, 1984, p. 4).

Goldhamer defined a number of preconditions that should be attached to the adviser's role: "friendship, admonition, information, education, analyses and advice, and special missions" (Goldhamer, 1978, p. 20). While he found that the demand for political experts varied with political structure, its size, and the relationships between the participants in the setting, his definition clearly emphasized the prime relationship between the adviser and the decision-maker.

He seemed to be fascinated by the presence of advisers within the social structure of a country (especially in ancient China, India, North Africa, and Italy) (Goldhamer, 1978, p. 20). Yet he began his book by noting that the term "adviser" lacks, "both in political practice and in political studies, a well established meaning" (Goldhamer, 1978, p. 3). He quotes Kautilya, an adviser to an Indian leader in the fourth century BC:

> This kind of seeking for advice is infinite and endless. The king should consult three or four ministers. A single minister proceeds willfully and without restraint ... But with three or four ministers he will not come to any serious grief, but will arrive at satisfactory results. (Goldhamer, 1978, p. 94)

3 The Whiz Kids and their Descendants

It was not surprising that the earliest people who identified themselves as policy analysts were found within the US Department of Defense (DoD). Individuals who had been systems analysts during World War II and the Korean War found themselves comfortable with the culture, the issues, and the language of the DoD.[3] Many of the staff had experience with RAND projects, and most of the staff were trained as economists. While they were working inside formal bureaucratic structures, many of them saw themselves as assigned to specific projects and operating more as time-limited consultants who did not perceive themselves to be permanent staff.

The introduction of the Planning, Programming, Budgeting System (PPBS) by Secretary of Defense Robert McNamara had clearly emerged from RAND experience and was eventually adopted government-wide (Radin, 2000, p. 14). Former RAND staff member Charles Hitch was hired to establish the DoD Systems Analysis unit with responsibility for the PPBS process. Goldhamer's perch in RAND contributed to his view that this activity was a part of the historical advising function that clearly crossed national boundaries (Radin, 2000, p. 15).

But the efforts of the Kennedy years were somewhat different from those of the past. New techniques were emerging from the natural sciences that led to positivism in the social sciences and normative economic reasoning that relied on the concept of a market. In addition, the computer technology that was available promised new methods of data analysis.

---

[3] By the mid-1970s, there was also a collection of policy analysis staff employed by several other federal agencies; the US Office of Economic Opportunity, the bureaucratic location of the War on Poverty, also was visible in terms of the development of the field.

While the activity in the DoD was viewed as an American effort, there was interest in its development beyond the US borders. Israeli economist Yehezkel Dror was one of the earliest advocates for the creation of policy analysis as a new profession. He was concerned that traditional economics did not push analysts to analyze alternative ways of dealing with policy issues (Dror, 1971).

At the same time, despite its focus on PPBS as a technical analytical methodology, there were other goals at play. The process allowed the Kennedy appointees to create opportunities for control by top agency officials over fragmented organizational and program units. It also was an attempt to improve efficiency in the way that resources were allocated and implemented. In addition, the PPBS process was based on a belief that an increased use of knowledge and information would produce better decisions. The term "Whiz Kids" was used to describe the small, elite corps of individuals in the DoD who had been trained as economists or operations researchers and who saw themselves as advisers to the cabinet secretary.

While crafted to meet the DoD's needs, President Lyndon Johnson saw the potential of the PPBS activity in other federal agencies (Radin, 2000, pp. 15–22). Something modeled on the DoD effort soon emerged in the Office of Economic Opportunity, the Department of Health, Education and Welfare, and the Department of the Interior. An older unit with similar responsibilities but different approaches had been established in 1947 in the Department of State.

3.1 Did the Early Whiz Kids Meet Goldhamer's Criteria?

The DoD PPBS staff members did meet many of Goldhamer's criteria for an adviser. They were advisers to leaders – not always the supreme leader, but clearly top leaders. They tended to be from less diverse elements of society, but clearly emerged from established professions. Women were rare in those staffs. While not always career bureaucrats, the advisers did place their work in a long-term time frame. They did have access to the leaders. They appeared to be aware of the importance of timing. They probably accentuated what Goldhamer called the "analytical mind" and were not likely to focus on the "intuitive mind" (Goldhamer, 1978, p. 5).

By October 1965, the DoD office that was established to carry out McNamara's analytical agenda moved toward its goal of "providing systematic, rational, and science-based counsel to decisionmakers. ... [It] included what has become the classic policy analysis litany: problem identification, the development of options or alternatives, the delineation of objectives and criteria, evaluation of these options, estimates of future effects, and – of course – recommendations for action" (Radin, 2000, p. 18). This office seemed to be an autonomous unit of skilled individuals who were not likely to have detailed knowledge of the substance of the policy assignments given to them.

Some of the original staff drew on their previous substantive experience involving defense issues, while others were more likely to focus less on the policy area than on the application of research methodologies and analytic methods to new areas.[4] The inchoate field became a combination of what some called "have analytic technique, will travel" staff, and it spread to a group of policy specialists beyond Defense. "Their specializations were in the techniques of analysis, not in the details of their application" (Radin, 2000, p. 16). President Johnson's focus on the possibilities attached to PPBS attracted attention to these efforts. It seemed that the policy analysis task was moving beyond a single analytic technique attached to the budget process. "Much still depended on the personal relationships between the analyst/adviser and the decision maker/ruler, but these organizations took their place in public, open, and legally constituted organizations" (Radin, 2000, p. 23).

But the focus of the activity was the formulation stage of the policy process. This was the stage of the process[5] where analysts would explore alternative approaches to "solve" a policy problem that had gained the attention of decision-makers and reached the policy agenda. In that sense, many analysts thought they had something resembling a tabula rasa (blank slate) before them.

But the slate didn't stay blank for long. The energetic Whizz Kids soon learned that important policy problems surfaced throughout Washington. Some were new issues but many touched existing programs and policies. The boundary expectations that the initial staff members had assumed were hard to maintain, and policy problems collided for attention with existing policies.

Laurence Lynn, an economist who had significant experience in the federal government, commented on the results of these early efforts:

> What seemed to be new ... was the self-conscious incorporation of policy analysis and policy analysts as a matter of principle into the central direction of large, complex government organizations. A new group of staff officers – policy analysts – answerable only to the organization's senior executive, were given privileged access to that executive and were empowered to speak for that executive in a variety of forums. (Quoted in Radin, 2000, p. 23)

---

[4] The expansion of PPBS beyond defense provided new experience for some of the DoD staff who were hired by other federal agencies. This was particularly true for economists who moved from DoD to the Department of Health, Education, and Welfare. In other cases, the staff expanded as it included others who specialized in the relevant policy area.

[5] Stages of the policy process were beginning to be defined. Most analysts used variations on the following: agenda setting, formulation, adoption, implementation, and evaluation.

3.2 Did the Original Expectations of the Policy Analyst's Role Continue?

While the policy analysis office inside the DoD continued largely along the original track that McNamara had supported, other players within the Washington cast of characters moved into this world. Staff who called themselves policy analysts were found everywhere in the nooks and crannies of Washington. They were not only in the top reaches of departments and agencies but were also found throughout the complexity of the Washington world, both inside and outside of government, where they appeared in multiple forms in congressional bodies such as the Congressional Research Service, the staffs of interest groups, and the think tanks that proliferated during this period.[6]

The efficiency goals that largely drew the original players trained as economists were often modified to meet political agendas or revised to reflect the issues that seemed important to staff who had different identities and training. It was not surprising that individuals trained as political scientists, sociologists, planners, or managers would raise different issues than had their predecessors. Organizations that focused on specific policy areas were attuned to the idiosyncrasies, histories, and cultures of that issue. And, increasingly, these new units in both the government and external groups saw their staff members as permanent careerists.

The results of these changes were chronicled by Arnold Meltsner in his volume, *Policy Analysts in the Bureaucracy* (1976). This book was based on 116 interviews conducted with federal policy analysts in 1970 and 1971, and documented the changes that were taking place during that period. Meltsner used these interviews to define four central factors: the analyst, the client, the organizational situation, and the policy area (Meltsner, 1976, p. 3). Meltsner had been a RAND staff member who took an academic career pathway, and his book provided a framework for others who were interested in these developments. While Meltsner continued Goldhamer's emphasis on the relationship between the analyst and the client, the other three factors he emphasized took a place within the broader political environment, as well as within the characteristics of the staff who were attracted to the field.

---

[6] By this period I had completed a Masters in American Studies and moved to Philadelphia to work for a labor union and become active in the civil rights movement there. By the time Johnson became president I had moved to Washington to work for the US Commission on Civil Rights. Thus, I was able to watch the expansion of some activities that became policy analysis from inside the federal government. I left the Civil Rights Commission to spend a year in London involved in immigration issues (i.e. the civil rights issues there). I returned to Washington as a consultant, but the day after Richard Nixon was elected I decided to apply for a PhD program in Social Policies Planning at the University of California at Berkeley.

Indeed, when APPAM was formed in 1978 and began to hold its annual research conferences, it fit Meltsner's perspective on the emerging field. The early conferences always included participation by individuals who were the clients of contemporary policy analysts and provided the basis for discussion of these relationships. Often, these clients were high-level public officials who received public attention for their policy work.[7] In addition, the structure of the conference was organized by subject or policy area. As such, it tends to follow the federal bureaucratic structure and minimize attention to issues that cross policy lines.

APPAM's conferences, publications, and structure gave new visibility to policy analysis activities. Most of the analytic activities that interested members originally dealt with national issues, but increasingly state and local efforts drew the attention of members. Although the organization included "management" in its title, the activities that were defined as "management" were usually found within substantive policy areas.

The organization reached out to the increasing number of think tanks, consulting firms, and universities and colleges that were exhibiting interest in the field. In recent years, policy analysts in the US federal system began to be increasingly located in national (and sometimes international) consulting firms that had long-term contracts with federal agencies.

The governance of the organization was relatively simple. Board members were elected to represent both academic and practitioner perspectives. Economists were often elected to official leadership positions but seemed less interested in governance issues than those with political science backgrounds. As the years progressed and the policy agenda changed, the size of staff employed by federal agencies sometimes grew in some political environments and sometimes decreased in others. Over the years, fewer analysts were employed directly by agencies and consulting firms "staffed" the federal agencies directly (and operated much like their bureaucratic colleagues). As a result, some critics argued that the major goal of the consulting firm was to renew its contracts.

4 Look to California: Aaron Wildavsky and Activity on the West Coast

Aaron Wildavsky was the first dean of the Berkeley Public Policy School, from 1969 to 1977. He published the first edition of *Speaking Truth to Power: The Art and Craft of Policy Analysis* in 1979 and concluded the book with an appendix

---

[7] This practice has been modified, and in contemporary years clients are rarely placed on conference-wide panels.

that discussed "Principles for a Graduate School of Public Policy." He published the second edition in 1987, with a new preface and a reprint of an article titled "The Once and Future School of Public Policy" that had originally appeared in *The Public Interest*, a quarterly public policy journal.

The years between the publication of the two books were seen by Wildavsky to represent dramatic changes in the field. His discussion of these changes sets the substantive context for the next part of the volume. The discussion of the School moved to the front of the second volume instead of the back. The following issues emerge from the contrast between Wildavsky's two books and provide a way of organizing many of the areas of conflict that are discussed in the remainder of this Element.

Around the same time that policy analysis was generating attention in Washington, DC, activity and interest of a somewhat different form was emerging from the University of California at Berkeley. Wildavsky, a professor of political science, was involved in research that seemed to challenge the RAND-influenced activities on the other side of the state from RAND. A first-generation American, Wildavsky wrote that his "activist temperament was unsuited to studying a political system at long range as if through the wrong end of a telescope" (Nienaber Clarke and Ingram, 2010, pp. 565–579).

Berkeley was certainly the place to be if one had an "activist temperament." The city witnessed a range of demonstrations during this period, focusing on race, the Viet Nam War, and a variety of other national, state, and local issues. Demonstrations on campus were so regular that one biologist argued that the trees on campus had learned to adapt to tear gas instead of oxygen.

One of Wildavsky's early interests was in the field of public budgeting. But his analysis in *The Politics of the Budgetary Process*, first published in 1964, brought a political scientist's perspective to an issue that had been largely ignored within the discipline. His research methodology did not rest on an auditor's green eye-shade or an economist's perspective, but was constructed based on interviews with the government bureaucrats and congressional staff involved in the budget process. He discovered that these staff members rarely had the opportunity to talk about their work.[8]

4.1 A School of Public Policy: Take One

It's not clear whether the PPBS staff working in Washington were really aware of the impact of Wildavsky's approach to budgeting. However, when his article "Rescuing Policy Analysis from PPBS" was published in the *Public*

---

[8] The volume was revised in multiple editions that reflected Wildavsky's commitment to incrementalism.

Administration Review in 1969, the consequences of his conclusions became apparent.

> Policy analysis aims at providing information that contributes to making an agency politically and socially relevant. Policies are goals, objectives, and missions that guide the agency. Analysis evaluates and sifts alternative means and ends in the elusive pursuit of policy recommendations. ... Because policy analysis is not concerned with projecting the status quo, but with tracing out the consequences of innovative ideas, it is a variant of planning. Complementing the agency's decision process, policy analysis is a tool of social change. (Wildavsky, 1969, p. 29)

Wildavsky's influence on the development of the world of the policy analyst went far beyond his research and writing. Although there were a few universities that had existing programs that promised to train something resembling policy analysts, the Berkeley experience that was led by Wildavsky (then the dean of the new public policy school) took the development of such a program very seriously.[9]

Wildavsky did not see the new school as simply an extension of existing academic fields. He saw the activity as something new and different. He believed that it would draw on existing programs, yet bridge them in original ways. Wildavsky described the early history of the Graduate School of Public Policy (formally established in 1968) as "the twilight world of policy analysis. Even if objectives are not multiple and conflicting, they are pretty sure to be vague" (Wildavsky, 1979, p. 405). It opened having admitted only Master's students, but planned to expand to doctoral students.

In 1979, Wildavsky published an edited volume entitled *Speaking Truth to Power: The Art and Craft of Policy Analysis*. It was issued just two years after he stepped down as the dean of the school. The volume was divided into four parts that, collectively, provided an extremely interesting picture of the academic dimensions of the field. He introduced the volume with a chapter entitled "Analysis as Art," and concluded it with a section called "Analysis as Craft." (Few thought of policy analysis as fitting into the art vs. craft dichotomy.) The four main sections of the book were "Resources versus Objectives," "Social Interaction versus Intellectual Cogitation," "Dogma versus Skepticism," and a final section that provided examples of policy analysis efforts. The appendix to the volume was entitled "Principles for a Graduate School of Public Policy," an essay that made Wildavsky's vision of the school explicit.

---

[9] Several foundations supported policy graduate programs at Berkeley, Harvard, Carnegie-Mellon, RAND Graduate Institute, and the universities of Michigan, Minnesota, Texas, and Pennsylvania.

The school that Wildavsky created was very unusual. It not only had a strong self-identification on the campus, but it also provided a setting for people from other parts of the campus and visitors to the campus to meet for lunch once a week. It seemed to communicate an agenda that moved across disciplinary lines, and even across the globe. Conversations in that setting were often focused on issues and behaviors that were not traditional research topics but represented important issues in the policy world, both locally and in the world of practice.[10] In addition, Wildavsky's constant companion in the school and on campus was his dog, Alice. Such a duo was not typical on campus.

Nienaber Clarke and Ingram commented that:

> We think it is no coincidence that a handful of scholars were drawn to what became the formal study of public policy during the 1960s. Politically, it was an unusually active period of government expansion into new realms of endeavor, and it was also a decade stained by violence and tragedy, both in the United States and abroad. Political debate and political conflict were endemic during those years, and very few scholars, especially in the social sciences, were not influenced by the momentous events occurring at that time (Nienaber Clarke and Ingram, 2010, p. 570).

The principles that Wildavsky outlined in the appendix seemed to depart from traditional academic planning. They involved predictable questions about the structure of the school, the faculty, the curriculum, and the administration. However, the answers were not always predictable because they were based on nontraditional expectations of the role of an academic unit in an academic field that was defined by its practice.

The Structure: Wildavsky attempted to make direct, 100 percent appointments in the school. No faculty member would have a joint appointment and thus would avoid what he called "two sets of quarrels." Programmatic structure would be shaped by physical space, but faculty from different disciplines would be encouraged to work together. There was only one path for admission to the PhD program: that was the MPP degree, with its required practical curriculum. That curriculum would be developed by the faculty.

The Faculty: Faculty would be economists interested in politics, political scientists interested in economics, and sociologists, lawyers, historians, philosophers, etc.,

---

[10] I was a PhD student in another department on campus and had arrived in Berkeley before the Policy School was in operation. It was clear that my interests were more compatible with the Policy School than the City and Regional Planning Department where I was formally enrolled. As a result I spent a lot of time attending classes in the Policy School, worked with faculty members there, and spent a semester in later years teaching in the school. In a sense, I was a participant-observer over the years.

interested in the work of their colleagues. Faculty should include people who had practical experience in doing, not merely talking about, policy analysis. Faculty would be encouraged to take frequent leave to actually practice policy analysis. Wildavsky had several maxims: hire analysts, not just economists; technical competence, statistical expertise, and formal elegance are desirable but not as important as the ability to conceptualize a solution; modeling is an art – hire an artist. Several of the original faculty members came from RAND and other sites of practice.

The Curriculum: Wildavsky believed that the core courses that were offered were school courses and belong to the school as an institution and not the individual instructor. He was wary about overloading the curriculum and sought what he called "creative redundancy" in the curriculum. The first year curriculum should be required and one should not worry about overemphasizing political and organizational factors. His advice was to take the high ground and emphasize moral aspects of public policy and emphasize analysis, not subject matter. He commented that "a student's resignation is also our failure" (Wildavsky, 1979, p. xxv). He wrote that unless a student obviously is wrong, we assume that, like the customer, he is always right. We want to teach students that their instructors also need to learn.

The Administration: Wildavsky commented that every effort should be made to create a nurturing environment in which students, staff, and faculty are assumed to be meritorious unless proven otherwise. He noted that an effort should be made to do something unless it is clearly contrary to school policy. He wrote that correcting errors when things go bad is easier if you help school members when things are good. He stated that his policy was to never have more rules than the number of people involved.

4.2 A School of Public Policy: Take Two

Eight years after the publication of the first edition, Wildavsky published a revised edition of the book.[11] That version of the book was issued ten years after he had stepped down as Dean and reflected a very different perspective on the institution and the policy analysis function. The essay that opened the volume was an unusual example of academic self-reflection as it reprinted an article that had been originally published in a 1985 issue of *The Public Interest* (no. 79 [Spring], pp. 25–41; reprinted in Wildavsky, 1987).

Wildavsky introduced the revised edition by emphasizing very different evaluations:

---

[11] While "speaking truth to power" has become a widely used phrase in the twenty-first century to describe policy analysis, Wildavsky's use of it in both editions was quite unusual.

I have two partially complementary and partially opposed views. One is that schools of public policy as they now exist will continue much as they are. The other is that social developments, particularly the growing polarization of elites, will substantially alter their character. In the course of elaborating both views, I shall post the usual questions: Where were these schools before? How did they get there? Where are they now? What will and/or should happen to them? (Wildavsky, 1987, p. xxii)

He commented:

The immediate impetus of graduate schools of public policy was undoubtedly the Great Society. Suddenly new major social programs were there, and almost as quickly, many of them were widely judged to have performed poorly. . . . Perhaps social science research is flawed so that negative rather than positive results are more likely to be reported. (Wildavsky, 1987, xiii)

During the years he served as dean, he also was an active policy analyst himself. He was someone who was often asked or invited by a wide variety of officials and administrators to take a look at their policy situations. Wildavsky always involved his students in these efforts, and a generation of policy analysts (and authors) was created as a result of these experiences.

While he commented on the changes in the larger environment, he also attempted to be realistic. He noted that people are difficult to change, that "no policy has effects in just one direction" (ibid.). He wrote:

In this introduction, I claim that there is a growing polarization of political elites, a polarization that must affect the ways in which analysis is done and analysts work. (ibid., xv)

While often described as a political cynic, he sometimes surprised his students and colleagues with his positions on issues. He wrote:

If I am correct in believing that American exceptionalism consists of the belief that equality of opportunity, rigorously pursued without monopoly or special privilege, would achieve an approximation of equal outcomes, it should have a broad application. (ibid., xvii)

He used the growing body of knowledge from evaluation to illustrate that when you subsidize something (like welfare), you are likely to get policies and institutions that "actually perpetuate institutions that oppressed the poor" (ibid., xxiv).

Wildavsky reflected on his experience of creating a school of public policy by commenting on what they were against as well as what they were for. These included the following:

This is not a school of public administration.[12]

This is not a school of foreign area studies.

The closest analogy to it is a school of business that has status, constituencies, support, and jobs for graduates.

It leads to work that will "set things right." (ibid., xxv)

That included improvement of the quality of the policy process. This latter item was not easy to define but it seemed to be similar to the role played by think tanks. Wildavsky looked to the development of the policy analysis involvement in evaluation but was doubtful about its utilization.[13]

Wildavsky commented on a number of elements in the social context. He continued to be critical of the PPBS tradition, and was skeptical about operations research and macro-economic approaches. He noted that "Schools of public policy needed some way to connect politics, economics, and organizations" (ibid., xxvii) and reminded his readers that the work of Harold Lasswell provided a focus on normative and problem-oriented issues (Laswell, 1970).

In a section of the introduction reprinting the article from *The Public Interest* entitled "Breaking the Bureaucratic Monopoly," Wildavsky suggested that the "demand for analysis depends on the desire for competition in the giving of advice." He continued:

> There must be more than one alternative; they must come from more than a single source; and there must be sufficient dispersion of power in society so that competing sources of advice have chance of being heard and acted upon. (Ibid.)

In a comment that seems to summarize his views about the potential of policy analysis, Wildavsky wrote:

> It is exactly intolerance for independent advice that has inhibited schools of public policy from starting in Europe. If you have hierarchical societies, if you have legitimated the idea of bureaucracy having a monopoly of expertise in policy areas, you will not look too favorably on the idea of think tanks. . . . Traditionally, the main characteristics of bureaucracy are seen as security of tenure and a monopoly of expertise. The policy analytic movement in America has weakened tenure and destroyed monopoly. (Ibid.)

Interestingly, Wildavsky commented that

> When ruling elites are dedicated to the expansion of government, graduates of schools of public policy would be an impediment. Instead of valuing government as the agency of first resort, they are likely to consider it

---

[12] This view may have contributed to an overemphasis on economics.

[13] This was also concern of a number of members of the evaluation community. See work of Carol Weiss (Weiss, 1983, 1992).

a vehicle of last resort. They will ask instead what incentives might be offered or disincentives removed to encourage others – private companies, community groups, semiofficial bodies – to take on the task. (Ibid., p. xxviii)

Wildavsky did find some positive results of the experience he was describing. He thought that students in a graduate school of public policy should learn how to collect data under difficult conditions, make sense of it, integrate it into organizational ambitions, and keep in touch with their clientele. He described the esprit de corp of analysts as thinking of alternatives, caring about results, and taking "a 'can do' attitude in a recalcitrant world." He described analysts as decentralizers (because of uncertainty, paucity of reliable data, and the absence of knowledge). He noted that "analysts do sing more than a single tune" (ibid., p. xxix) and thus are aware of the defects of decentralization. But, at the same time, they are also skeptical of centralization.

Wildavsky also noted that schools of public policy in the United States flourish. As he looked around him, he wasn't sure how many schools actually existed, but he wrote that they have similar curricula that include microeconomics, quantitative modeling, political and organizational analyses, and either a practicum on some area of policy or a practicum combined with an effort to teach "political economy" – "that is principles for or against government intervention in different contexts" (ibid., p. xxx).

While these elements were important, Wildavsky wrote:

> More important than their curriculum, in my opinion, is their methods. From the first week, students are placed in an active position. They analyze, grub for data, reformulate problems, write and write again to communicate with clients. Fieldwork is their forte. An analyst with clean hands … is a contradiction in terms. (ibid.)

Moving into the field attracted more diverse categories of students than were usually found in some traditional political science classes. Wildavsky's students and collaborators represented groups that had been underrepresented in the past, especially women and students of color. Observers sometimes noticed that issues were brought to the policy agenda that had rarely found their way there in the past.

He acknowledged the differences among the policy schools but commented that the differences were marginal (such as substituting the term "management" for "public administration"). He noted that "Teaching leadership, like inculcating entrepreneurship, is difficult, perhaps impossible, to do. No one knows how to teach others to become creative. Going the other way, however, a technocratic approach – the manager's task is to achieve clear, consistent, and preordained objectives – is rejected by adherents of public management" (ibid.).

Asking himself how successful graduate schools of public policy have been, Wildavsky's response was mixed. By any reasonable indicator of success in this work, he noted that the students evoked dedication from the faculty, the capacity to attract talented students, the willingness of people to do research, the demand for this service in society, and seemed to be recession-proof (ibid., p. xxxi) But he asked himself: are our graduates "doing right?" (ibid., p. xxxiii). "They love to do good but discover that they (or the project on which they are working) are doing poorly" (ibid., p. xxxv).

He found that this institution was intrinsically American because it has such a restricted ideological base. Unlike Europe, America lacks conflict between socialist and capitalist parties, fails to question economic and political competition, and is often seen as ideologically homogeneous. Yet Americans don't avoid unresolved conflicts. He notes that they are incrementalists, at the margins, and that students are likely to be liberal and change oriented.

He wrote:

> The fiction of analytic impartiality has blinded Americans to the influential policy analysis that is done in Europe, not because of its uneven quality but because of its location in interest groups and political parties. By making policy subordinate to politics, Europeans prefer to give up efficiency for legitimacy. (ibid., p. xxxii)

Wildavsky summarized his views about the attributes of schools of public policy with a few terms. Some of these terms reflected an evaluative posture while others were simply descriptive. They are incrementalist. They are parochial. They train empiricists and mini-economists. Their aim is completed work (which includes acceptance by the client organization, its conversion into action, its evaluation, and its modification) (ibid., p. xxxiii).

As that doesn't always occur, he lists some specific areas for change (which, inevitably, will be incremental). This includes coursework on moral problems of public policy in which differences in values become apparent. Such a discussion would illustrate "the range of agreement in society" (ibid.) and refer to the social revolution of power between men and women, white and black, parents and children. It would also refer to issues that deal with social conservatism: "Though egalitarian and fundamentalist elites are alike in their fervor, they differ in the direction of their passions" (ibid.).

He notes that schools of public policy were never designed to deal with large-scale social change and concludes that there is no market for radical change. But "there is a market among activists, political leaders and media personalities who shape the consideration of issues" (ibid.).

Wildavsky concludes his 1985 essay by asking "Can the center hold?" He asks his readers to consider ways in which evidence matters (and where polarized elites talk and make sense to one another.) The incrementalist in him writes that "schools of public policy should remain much as they are today" (ibid., p. xxxvii). Yet should polarization grow, then other possibilities emerge. It is hard to be clear about Wildavsky's own policy agenda.

He suggests several topics: new methodological concerns, an interest in the relationship between facts and values, and reexamination of political subjects (such as democracy, consensus, authority, legitimacy). That might lead to a joining between political economy and political culture and an explicit treatment of values built into the US system.[14]

He concludes his essay in a way that suggests that he has significantly changed his approach to the field: "Problem solving will still be an essential characteristic of policy analysis, but it will be joined by its twin, problem finding – the study of what comes to be defined as a problem of public policy for adherents of different political cultures" (ibid., p. xxxviii).

4.3 Had Wildavsky Really Changed his Views?

One might have expected some of Wildavsky's students and colleagues to respond to the gap that seemed to have been created by his leap into a different set of issues and concerns. It almost seems as if his commitment to the field in which he invested incredible time and intellectual power was diminishing. Indeed, at least some of his students found that Aaron's interests were less focused on policy analysis and more on traditional political science issues. A number of those students and colleagues concentrated on specific policy issues (e.g. environmental issues, health policy, education systems), on classic concerns about changes in the stages of the policy process, or on the use of new methods to explore issues.

4.4 How Should Wildavsky's Heritage Represent his Complex Perspectives?

What can a reader glean from the two descriptions of the policy analysis field that Wildavsky actually produced? They do contain some similarities, but they more than hint that the relatively short life of the field had already produced differences between the two comments. It is clear that Wildavsky was aware

---

[14] His interest in the concept of political culture had been present in much of his work throughout his career. His early examination of the source of personal preferences uncovered links to values and beliefs that were expressed by different cultural types that drew on Weberian ideal types (egalitarian, hierarchical, individualistic, and fatalistic) (see Mary Douglas and Aaron Wildavsky, 19833).

that the policy analysis of the 1970s was different than what he found ten years later. His modifications of his original views made his contribution to the field more difficult to define.

And the question can be expanded: Did Wildavsky's insights seem to be moving toward the definitions of the role of the policy analyst that have emerged in the twenty-first century? Would he have focused on comparative approaches to policy analysis? Would he have attempted to combine advocacy with his past work? He seemed to intertwine his role as a citizen with his role as a player in the analytic process. Would he have focused on specific analytic techniques and opportunities created by new technological developments? We know that a number of his students were attracted to focusing on environmental issues and continued their careers in that direction.

His early death in 1993 makes our answers speculative. Given Wildavsky's role in the development of the original policy analysis field, one might have expected his students and colleagues to fill in the missing pieces of its development. Perhaps the best evidence concerning Wildavsky's predilections can be inferred from publications produced by his colleagues and his doctoral students during the years after his death.

Arnold Meltsner described the process of advising as analogous to a theatrical production, with the role of the analyst determined by issues defined by the client (Meltsner, 1990) Meltsner emphasized the importance of the relationship between the analysis and the client.

Another colleague, Eugene Bardach, turned his class syllabus into a textbook that continues to be one of the major sources in the field. Bardach was known for an exercise that required students to develop a policy analysis in 48 hours. Described as a handbook, the volume is titled *A Practical Guide for Policy Analysis: The EightFold Path to More Effective Problem Solving* (Bardach, 2016). Until the fifth edition, the 200 page book did not even mention the role of the client in the policy analysis process (and when it appeared, it was an appendix to the book). Did that suggest that the relationship to a decision-maker-client was not important?

Two of Wildavsky's earliest PhD students published an extensive text on policy analysis in 1989. They found themselves teaching courses on policy analysis "without what we considered to be fully adequate for an introductory course at the graduate level" (Weimer and Vining, 1989, p. ix). The Weimer and Vining volume is now in its sixth edition, is more than 400 pages long, and emphasizes policy analysis as a client-driven enterprise. Both Weimer and Vining continue to publish work today, and have focused on what it means for a policy analyst to work with or without a client.

Iris Geva-May came to Berkeley from Israel to work with Wildavsky on a book that sought to detail ways to operationalize policy analysis. The book that they had worked on together was drafted when he became ill with cancer but published (with his family's agreement) under her name (Geva-May, 1997). She also wrote about policy analysis as a clinical profession and tended to think about clients as being psychosocial. She defined policy analysis as a clinical professional field like medicine, psychology, or law.

Other Wildavsky students or colleagues focused on issues that emerged in the context of specific analytic work, particularly questions related to policy design,[15] new approaches to benefit–cost analysis,[16] implementation,[17] and experiences with policy and program evaluation.[18] Some of them continued to travel along the path of dualities and complexities that characterized much of Wildavsky's work, but others focused on a single task, value, or problem. His own observations seemed always to carry the insights of a political scientist observing a world of contradictions.

5 Section Two: What Helps Explain the Changes in the Definition of Policy Analysis?

There are a number of elements that can be drawn from Wildavsky's complex heritage that can help contemporary policy analysts identify the roots of the various definitions of policy analyst that they are likely to be using today. I present them as questions that are answered implicitly by most people who have identified themselves as students of policy analysis. For some, the answers are obvious – indeed, even implicit, in the term *policy analysis.*

As the field developed, the answers to these questions seemed to move along a pathway. Some of these elements are clear and lead to a specific model of the policy analyst, while others are less obvious or actually contain conflicting elements within that or another model. As a result, it is not surprising that the policy analysis field is characterized by dissention and definitions that evade clarity. Many of the answers are not unique to policy analysis and may be found in other disciplines. But they appear to continue to be unsettled in the policy analysis field and have lead to different generational approaches to these topics.

The following five sets of questions are relevant to this quest. Many of them have their clear roots in Wildavsky's work, but they also allow us to expand to developments that have occurred since his death. As I have noted, Wildavsky's style and creativity rarely led him to an answer that was clear and permanent. Indeed, his commitment to the development of alternative options was evidence of his attention to the possibility of change.

---

[15] Helen Ingram.   [16] David Weimer and Aidan Vining.   [17] The late Jeffrey Pressman.
[18] The late Carol Weiss.

1. Is there a difference between policy analysis and policy research? Does the difference focus largely on the presence of a client?
2. Did the move of policy analysis from its origins in the world of practice to its base in the academic world make a difference? If so, what changes accompanied that shift?
3. Did changes in both the internal and external environments of policy analysis make a difference? These could have focused on the effects of constant change, globalization, differentiation between public and private sectors, and organization structure (e.g. networks, shared powers).
4. Were there changes in the repertoire of analytic techniques used by policy analysts? Where did new techniques come from (e.g. other disciplines, private sector, data sources)? Did the focus on evidence make any difference?
5. What values structured the analytic process (e.g. efficiency, equity, effectiveness)? Were values built into some policy issues and policy cultures? Was the search for theory related to tendencies to define one-size-fits-all situations?

6 Question One: The Differences Between Analysis and Research

Is there a difference between policy analysis and policy research? Does the difference focus largely on the presence of a client?

Unlike most academic and research fields, the policy analysis field did not start out operating as an independent and separate effort. In fact, by definition the field involves a relationship (or at least a conversation between an analyst and a decision-maker or a decision-making process) (Radin, 2019, p. 9). Some have actually characterized this as a transfer of information from someone who is viewed as an expert on a specific topic to someone else who has been charged with making a decision about something related to that topic.

The earliest US literature describing the formal policy analysis profession emphasized the role played by the client in defining the relationship between the analyst and the client. And it was not surprising that this individual was expected to be found in the bureaucratic halls of the US federal government. Unlike other professionals, the term "client" was used to define the users and not the beneficiaries of the analytic work (Meltsner, 1976, p. 201).

From the first edition of their book, Weimer and Vining highlighted the differences between policy analysis and other related areas. See Table 1

There are many different ways to define the basic structure of policy analysis. From the beginning of the professional field – despite its links to systems

Table 1 Policy Analysis in Perspective

Paradigms	Major Objectives	"Client"	Common Style
Academic social science research	Construction of theories for understanding society	"Truth" as defined by the disciplines; other scholars	Rigorous methodology to construct and test theories; often retrospective
Policy research	Prediction of impacts of changes in "variables" that can be altered by government	Actors in the policy arena; the related disciplines	Applications of formal methodology to policy-relevant questions; predictions of consequences
Classical planning	Defining and achieving desirable future state of society	The "public interest" as professionally defined	Established rules and professional norms; specification of goals and objectives
The "old" public administration	Efficient execution of programs established by political processes	The mandated program	Managerial and legal
Journalism	Focusing public attention on societal problems	General public	Descriptive
Policy analysis	Analyzing and presenting alternatives available to political actors for solving public problems	A specific decision-maker or collective decision-maker	Synthesis of existing research and theory to estimate consequences of alternative decisions

Adapted from Weimer and Vining, 1992, Second Edition p. 4

analysis and other developments in economics – there was a tension between two cultures: the culture of analysis and the culture of politics. In spite of the assumption that analysts would be governed by the norms of neutrality and objectivity attached to research norms, it was clear that clients would raise political issues.

The initial image of the profession that began in the US DoD in the 1960s defined clients as individuals who were identifiable through their job title and defined responsibilities. The hierarchical structure of the federal bureaucracy and the culture of the military led to an emphasis on the cabinet secretary of the DoD as the client. That client was assumed to be a man who appeared to understand both the culture of analysis as well as the culture of politics. Meltsner quoted one of his informants in *Policy Analysts in the Bureaucracy*, in his chapter entitled "Clients": "He's the man you work for. . . . He's the man who tells you to proceed with the project or approves your analytical recommendations" (Meltsner, 1976, chapter 6, p. 201).

Yet Meltsner found that a variety of client–analyst relationships emerged in his interviews.

About half of the respondents thought that clients would use an analysis. and half did not expect that analysts intended the clients to use the analysis. Interaction between the two was extremely variable and direct relationships between analysts and clients were rare (ibid., p. 203.) After a decade or so of functioning, Meltsner found that analysts varied tremendously and were hard to characterize (Meltsner 1976, p. 48). Despite this, he continued to emphasize the role of the client.

When Arnold Meltsner revised his book in 1986, he included developments that indicated some significant changes had taken place in the issues that were defined by clients. Some of these changes reflected the addition of new types of clients and the interests they brought to the process. While bureaucratic clients remained, he noted that the client field grew to include legislative groups, interest groups, think tanks, and other nongovernmental organizations. Meltsner commented on clients' lack of trust in analysis and noted that when clients "become distrustful of advising, they are likely to cut themselves off from new and fresh sources of information" (Meltsner, 1986, p. 371).

In addition, clients not only emerged as individuals but as institutional processes of governing (planning, budgeting, regulation development, legislative drafting) as well as maintenance of an organization. Increasingly, clients were including policy analysis as a part of all the stages of the policy process. The earlier emphasis on the policy formulation stage of the policy process was expanded to include policy adoption, policy implementation, and policy evaluation (Radin, 2013a, chapter 2). In addition, by the end of the twentieth century the field had moved beyond the national level to include clients at the state and local government levels. This was particularly important in program areas where implementation authority funded by the national government was at the discretion of state or local agencies. At that point, there appeared to be little interest in an activity that was termed "policy analysis" beyond US borders.

As a result, the classic role conflict between a client and an analyst was not only defined in terms of personal roles, expectations, and attributes, but was also linked to the complexity of the policy process and the conflict between administration and politics. At that point it seemed to be an American activity, even though it had other antecedents.

Many clients of analysts continue to be identified because of their positions as individuals with formal authority who are located on the top rungs of public organizations. But other shifts occurred in the policy world that changed the concept of "client." Increasingly, participants in the policymaking world found that the formal hierarchical bureaucratic structure does not always describe the decision-making process in a governmental agency.

Several other issues have made the contemporary definition of a client extremely complex. There is frequently a conflict between those who approach the policy process as a substantive activity that highlights the quality of public services and those who see it only as the allocation of budget resources. It is not always clear how a client balances those two imperatives because many government structures try to keep the two functions separate. This proves to be difficult as political polarization has increased through the shifts that occur as a result of elections and staff changes.

In addition, the effects of globalization in many policy areas have complicated both the expectations of the client as well as the capacities of the analyst. Given the growth of global relationships, policy participants are likely to be more aware of the activity of multinational organizations and the differences between the participants who emerge from different cultures and structures. These include types of policy issues, diverse relationships between analysts and clients, types of analysis required, time frames, stages of the policy process, structures of policy analysis, the boundaries between policy analysis and management, the relationship between career and political actors, skills required, and – perhaps most importantly – the structure of the government. The US system of shared power between the branches of government as well as its structure of federalism creates a map of actors with multiple but limited authority.

As a result of these changes as well as the acknowledgment of complexity, ambiguity about the client's role and expectations has increased. This may be related to the increase in informal processes that mask the certainty that is often assumed to be attached to formal processes. Analysts search for new ways to enter the system at the same time that the formal hierarchical structures do not encourage paths that provide an opening to enter the formal authority.

As the years went by, the field did seem to be moving toward a professional identity for policy analysts. Schools and departments of public policy spread across the country. Some were freestanding while others were parts of public administration, political science, or business programs. Some academic programs were known for their interest in specific policy areas, and joint degree programs became more common. Creation of the professional organization (the APPAM) yielded yearly research conferences that provided an opportunity for both academics and practitioners to present their findings. Curricula requirements and subject offerings tended to move in similar directions. MPP programs usually had quantitative analysis requirements, policy process courses, and applied projects that emphasized application rather than theory. Faculty tended to come from more traditional academic fields, and in the early years many of them came to the academy with practitioner experience in the growing policy analysis field. However, as the programs proliferated, fewer faculty had practitioner experience before coming to the academy. Faculty varied in terms of the impact of this loss.

At the same time, many issues remained unresolved, or at least unclear. Both efforts labeled as policy analysis and those called fiscal decision-making seemed to be important, but the two approaches continued to have an uneasy relationship. When analysts were usually located in organizational units attached to the highest levels of a department or agency they found themselves separated from staff units charged with operating responsibilities. That was particularly difficult when policy analysts were focusing on implementation alternatives and strategies.

Conflicting advice emanated from Meltsner and from Israeli political scientist Yehezkel Dror. Dror called for broadening the scope of the analyst's role beyond the use of technical skills to encompass the organizational and political realities that made up "the public interest" (Dror 1971, quoted in Radin, 2013a, pp. 26–27). It was not easy to calculate "the public interest" in the diverse and fragmented American society but, despite that, policy analysts grew in both numbers and visibility. They showed up in middle and lower levels in the bureaucracy and became increasingly socialized to the policy cultures and political structures in which they were dealing.

By the early years of the twenty-first century, Vining and Weimer provided an alternative definition of policy analysis that moved beyond the earlier definitions offered by Meltsner and Dror. It required both a client and a substantive focus on advancing social values. They wrote:

We distinguish it [policy analysis] from policy research, which shares the substantive focus but not the requirement of a specific client, and from political/organizational, or stakeholder, analysis, which has a specific client but an instrumental rather than substantive focus. ... We recognize policy process as distinct from, but nevertheless, potentially informative for political/organizational and policy analysis. (Vining and Weimer, 2010)

Yet few of the academic programs that identified themselves as "public policy schools" agreed with the Vining–Weimer differentiation between research and analysis. More were likely to fudge the differences between the two approaches and could not define themselves within only one of the quartiles of the table that Vining and Weimer included in their article (see Table 2).

While Vining and Weimer argued that there was significant difference between the client focus attached to policy analysis and the academic/societal focus that defined the policy research approach, that differentiation is not always acknowledged within the community of people who call themselves policy analysts.

For some analysts, the responsibilities attached to the relationship with a client seemed to be a departure from the values of objectivity and neutrality built into the research role. It opened the door to conceptualizing their role as an advocate, but with values embedded in the analyst's personal perspective. It was not always clear where the client fitted in.

Many clients of analysts continued to be identified because of their formal and public positions. It was assumed that clear authority was attached to their role (something that was more likely in military organizations than in domestic agencies). Increasingly, participants in the policymaking world found that the formal hierarchical bureaucratic structure did not always describe the decision-making process in a governmental agency. Nor was it limited to players inside the system. Shared authority was found to be more common, and thus a single individual client did not always have the sole authority to act on analytic advice. Multiple decision-makers are likely to have a role in such a process and can be seen as legitimate actors in the decision-making process. These actors may involve players across different levels of government who have a legitimate role in the policy process.

As a result, the term "policy analyst" continues to confuse many people in academic programs (both faculty and students) as well as in the world of practice. Most of the individuals who are viewed as analysts represent quite different examples of the clear typology proposed by Vining and Weimer. Just as clients/decision-makers come to their role wearing very different clothing with diverse expectations about their use of analytic work, analysts also differ in terms of their expectations.

Table 2 Taxonomy of "Policy Analysis"

	CLIENT VERSUS SOCIETAL FOCUS	
Substantive Policy/Policy Analytic Focus	**Client Focus** **Policy Analysis (narrowly defined)**	**Academic/Social Focus** **Policy Research/Policy Sciences**
	Problem-solving focus	Social science research on policy problems
	Economics preeminent	Policy problem discovery/ exploration
	Comprehensive: problem analysis (market & government failure, synthesis, solution analysis (alternatives, goals, assessment)	Solution (policy) Discovery/exploration
		Broad range of social sciences, but economics, political science dominate
	Goals clear, or at least emergently clear; efficiency (cost–benefit) or efficiency, equity, government revenue-expenditure (multi-goal)	Partial or fragmentary (in terms of policy problem) Goals contestable

SUBSTANTIVE VERSUS PROCESS FOCUS

Policy Process Focus	Political/Organizational Analysis (or Stakeholder Analysis)	Policy Process Research
	Political, organizational, and interorganizational analysis (including networks)	All social science research, but dominated by political science research
	Relevant for both adoption and implementation	Distributional and redistributional focus (iron triangles, etc.)
	Strategic client focus	Theory somewhat contestable: interest-group theory, advocacy coalition, path dependency, etc., but converging on contingent and comprehensive theory
	Often informal and unwritten	
	Primarily descriptive and predictive, rather than normative: goal is adoption and implementation	

From Vining and Weimer, 2010, p. 50

While the Vining and Weimer taxonomy is very useful, it does ignore another element in conceptualizing the role of the policy analyst. There is a complicated relationship between the analyst's personal values and expectations and those embedded in the activities expected to be undertaken within the position itself (Radin, 2019).

6.1 Clients: A Moving Target

The earliest literature in the United States describing the formal policy analysis profession emphasized the role played by the client in defining the relationship between the analyst and the client. And it was not surprising that this individual was expected to be found in the bureaucratic halls of the US federal government. Unlike other professionals, the term "client" was used to define the users and not the beneficiaries of the analytic work (Meltsner, 1976, p. 201). While the historical concept of the "client" reached beyond a governmental bureaucracy, in the past it emphasized individuals found in positions of authority and power in royal, hereditary, religious, and other settings.

From the beginning of the professional field – despite its links to systems analysis and other developments in economics – there was a tension between two cultures: the culture of analysis and the culture of politics. Despite the acceptance that analysts would be governed by the norms of neutrality and objectivity, it was clear that clients would raise political issues. As Deborah Stone noted, "Reasoned analysis is necessarily political. It always involves choices to include some things and exclude others and to view the world in a particular way when other visions are possible" (Stone, 1997, p. 375). Thus the presence of the client embedded the political perspective that reflected the world of the decision-maker.

The initial image of the profession that began in the US DoD in the 1960s defined clients as individuals who were identifiable through their job title and formal responsibilities. The hierarchical structure of the federal bureaucracy and the culture of the military led to an emphasis on the cabinet secretary of the DoD. That client was someone who appeared to understand both the culture of analysis and the culture of politics.

Meltsner found that a variety of client–analyst relationships emerged in his interviews. About half of the respondents thought that clients would use an analysis, and half did not expect that analysts intended the clients to use the analysis. Interaction between the two was extremely variable and direct relationships between analysts and clients were rare (Meltsner, 1976, p. 203.) After a decade or so of functioning, Meltsner found that analysts varied tremendously and were hard to characterize (ibid., p. 48). Yet, he continued to emphasize the role of the client.

When Meltsner revised his book in 1986, he included developments that indicated that some significant changes had taken place in the issues that were defined by clients. Some of these changes reflected the addition of new types of clients and the interests they brought to the process. While bureaucratic clients continued, he noted that the client field grew to include legislative groups, interest groups, and other nongovernmental organizations. Meltsner commented on clients' lack of trust in analysis and noted that when clients "become distrustful of advising, they are likely to cut themselves off from new and fresh sources of information" (Meltsner, 1986, p. 71).

For some, however, it was impossible to think about policy analysis without conceptualizing it as a process that involved two players (Radin, 1997, p. 204). While many tend to look at the worlds of practice and theory as two very separate cultures that are destined to maintain their distance, a field such as policy analysis cannot survive without finding ways to bring the insights of both cultures together, or at least to acknowledge their differences as well as their shared areas.

It is a field that encompasses the expectations and demands of both cultures. However, clearly there are real differences between the two worlds. Practitioners focus on application of knowledge, look to define and solve problems, and emphasize the uniqueness of the situation before them. They operate in a short time framework; acknowledge conflicts of values, goals, purposes, and interests; focus on uncertainty, disorder, and indeterminacy; and emphasize complexity. Researchers seek to build theory, generate knowledge, generalize patterns, simplify, work in the long term, and try to minimize uncertainty, disorder, and indeterminacy. Both of these roles and all of these elements are legitimate, but it is difficult and challenging to find a way to acknowledge that legitimacy and to find ways that allow the two approaches to complement one another. Nonetheless, that challenge is important and worth pursuing (Radin, 2013b, pp. 1–7).

In other cases, these multiple players move beyond governmental entities to involve nongovernmental agencies who are linked together in networks that may be both formal and informal in nature. Often these networks contain a mixture of actors (from both firms and nonprofit organizations) with different resources and diverse perspectives on an issue. Several other issues have made the contemporary definition of a client extremely complex. There is frequently a conflict between those who approach the policy process as a substantive activity that highlights the quality of public services and those who see it only as the allocation of budget resources. It is not always clear how a client balances those two imperatives because many government structures try to keep the two functions separate. This proves to be difficult as political polarization has increased through the shifts that occur as a result of elections and staff changes.

In addition, the effects of globalization in many policy areas have complicated both the expectations of the client as well as the capacities of the analyst. Given the growth of global relationships, policy participants are likely to be more aware of the activity of multinational organizations and the differences between the participants who emerge from different cultures and structures. These include types of policy issues, diverse relationships between analysts and clients, types of analysis required, time frames, stages of the policy process, structures of policy analysis, the boundaries between policy analysis and management, the relationship between career and political actors, skills required, and – perhaps most importantly – the structure of the government.

Because of their personal experience as practitioners, the founders of our field drew on the insights of both cultures and minimized their often conflicting demands. Indeed, this combination brought forth the outlines of an exciting and important field. While Wildavsky was not the only player in the process of defining the original field, he seemed to be comfortable in both cultures. Today, however, it seems to me that the worlds have parted and we seem to be operating in parallel universes.

In addition, clients not only emerged as individuals but as institutional processes of governing (planning, budgeting, regulation development, legislative drafting) as well as maintenance of an organization. Increasingly, clients were including policy analysis as a part of all the stages of the policy process. The earlier emphasis on the policy formulation stage was expanded to include policy adoption, policy implementation, and policy evaluation (Radin, 2013a, chapter 2). In addition, by the end of the twentieth century the field had moved beyond the national level to include clients at state and local government levels. This was particularly important in program areas where implementation authority funded by the national government was within the discretion of state or local agencies. There appeared to be little interest in an activity that was termed "policy analysis" but crafted to meet unique US circumstances.

As a result, the classic role conflict between a client and an analyst was not only defined in terms of personal roles, expectations, and attributes, but was also linked to the complexity of the policy process and the conflict between administration and politics. When this was realized (at that point in its development) it seemed to be an American activity even though it had other antecedents. The complex demands that were made of both the client and the analyst led many of them to operate in separate tracks and also to deny the legitimacy of the other.

In other cases, these multiple players move beyond governmental entities to involve nongovernmental agencies who are linked together in networks that may be both formal and informal in nature. Often these networks contain a mixture of actors (both from profit and nonprofit groups) with different resources and diverse perspectives on an issue. In these cases it becomes quite difficult to define the perspective of "the client" when the "client" is actually a complex organization where players do not always want to be clear about their goals and expectations and instead like the flexibility that accompanies uncertain relationships. The increase in contracting-out activities that traditionally have been done by government employees brings new players to roles in these networks even though they may not have formal authority.

Several other issues have made the contemporary definition of a client extremely complex. There is frequently a conflict between those who approach the policy process as a substantive activity that highlights the quality of public services and those who see it only as the allocation of budget resources. It is not always clear how a client balances those two imperatives since many government structures try to keep the two functions separate. This proves to be difficult as political polarization has increased through the shifts that occur as a result of elections and staff changes.

In addition, the effects of globalization in many policy areas have complicated both the expectations of the client as well as the capacities of the analyst. Given the growth of global relationships, policy participants are likely to be more aware of the activity of multinational organizations and the differences between the participants who emerge from different cultures and structures. These include types of policy issues, diverse relationships between analysts and clients, types of analysis required, time frames, stages of the policy process, structures of policy analysis, the boundaries between policy analysis and management, the relationship between career and political actors, skills required, and – perhaps most importantly – the structure of the government.

As a result of these changes, ambiguity about the client's role and expectations has increased. This may be related to the increase in informal processes that mask the certainty that is often attached to formal processes. Analysts search for new ways to enter the system at the same time that the formal hierarchical structures do not encourage paths that provide an opening to enter the formal authority.

By the end of the twentieth century, the list of skill areas that were thought to be relevant to a skilled policy analyst had become more extensive. Meltsner's dichotomy between technical skills and political skills was relatively simple. The technical skills he found had emerged from economics and systems analysis and the political skills emphasized the realities faced by the relevant clients. The newer group of skills reached beyond those used in the search for the formulation and adoption of new policies and moved into implementation and evaluation stages of the policy process that often included existing policies and programs.

6.2 The Analyst: Expectations and Constraints

For more than fifty years, both academics and practitioners have tried to find a way to define the field that we call policy analysis. Unlike fields such as economics, political science, public management, and sociology, it has been more difficult to agree on the intellectual location of the field or what it actually accomplishes. In that sense, Wildavsky's ambiguities about the field are not surprising.

Although the field of policy analysis had its original roots in the world of decision-making and practice, its development over a half century has created an academic field that is located around the globe. It is found in many different institutions of higher education, is the main subject of a number of journals and other publications, is the focus of national and international organizations, and continues to generate debate about the parameters of its research subjects and methodologies. Examination of articles in what are viewed as policy journals uncovers a wide range of methods and approaches to the topic.

But much of the literature focuses on the analytical techniques employed by the analyst, not on the process of interacting with the client. In other cases, these multiple players move beyond governmental entities to involve nongovernmental agencies who were linked together in networks that may be both formal and informal in nature. Often, these networks contain a mixture of actors (from both profit and nonprofit groups) with different resources and diverse perspectives on an issue. In these cases it becomes quite difficult to define the perspective of "the client" when the "client" is actually a complex organization wherein players do not always want to be clear about their goals and expectations and instead like the flexibility that accompanies uncertain relationships. The increase in contracting-out activities that traditionally have been done by government employees brings new players to roles in these networks even though they may not have formal authority.

There is also a lack of clarity about its dimensions as a part of the field of practice. Jobs with the label "policy analyst" can be found, but they are often subsections of jobs in the category of program or budget analyst. While the early years of the field assumed that "policy analysts" were always found in bureaucratic government jobs, current job advertisements suggest that positions in the field are also found in a wide range of nonprofit and for-profit settings, as well as in legislative organizations. In some cases, while jobs are called "policy analyst" positions, the employment requirements suggest that organizations are looking for staff who might be more accurately defined as "policy advocates" rather than "policy analysts".

There was not a single definition of the term "policy analyst" that would be agreed to by the players in either the academic or practitioner settings. The early years of the field that began in the US DoD in the 1960s appeared to indicate a setting that may have given the original policy analysts an illusion of agreement on the definition of the job. During those early years, it seemed to be possible to reach agreement that the early clients of the new process were high-level officials in the government who sought advice on the development of new policies. And the clients were often familiar with the analytic techniques that the analysts were using.

Similarly, it was possible to attain agreement on the role and background of those who were then defined as policy analysts. They were economists who were likely to have a specialty in systems analysis and were likely to draw on their skill in benefit–cost analysis. They were familiar with the PPBS: the decision allocation process that allowed them to link planning and program analysis to the budget process. The original group was composed of individuals who had worked for the RAND Corporation in Santa Monica, California, on defense-related issues. Some of them saw their careers as in-and-out consultants, while others expected to craft a career around their government service. Many of them seemed confident that the analytical approaches used in Defense would be effective in other federal agencies and applicable to other policy problems and issues.

This sense of optimism also reflected the views of the Kennedy administration. The "New Frontier" had attracted a group of experts to the shores of the Potomac who saw the possibilities in the new activity. Although this optimism was challenged by the assassination of John F. Kennedy and the attention to the war in Viet Nam, Lyndon Johnson was especially intrigued by the possibilities raised by these DoD experts and chose to require that the technique be used throughout the government. Those expectations were rarely met.

Arnold Meltsner, the author of *Policy Analysts in the Bureaucracy* and a former staffer at RAND, moved to the faculty at the University of California at Berkeley when the Graduate School of Public Policy (now the Goldman School) was created. In 1976, Meltsner became the first academic to attempt to capture the work, views, and limitations of the individuals who were then being called "policy analysts" (Meltsner, 1976, p. 4). In many ways, his interviews with these individuals emphasized their unique qualities. He wrote about the impact of their training, formal education, beliefs about reality, and motivations to make an impact on policymaking. He distinguished between analysts who were technicians, politicians, or entrepreneurs and emphasized that policy analysts often set their own expectations (ibid).

As it developed, the field itself was experiencing growing pains, and definition of success in the practice of policy analysis was not always obvious or agreed upon. Several questions were difficult to answer. Was success the ability to convince the client/decision-maker to adopt your recommendation? Was an analyst successful when he or she helped the client understand the complexity and dimensions of a policy choice? Was the analyst successful when the work that was done was publishable and approved by one's peers within the profession? The norms behind each of these questions suggested that policy analysis was a field that embraced the values of science, neutrality, and research at the same time that it also embraced pragmatic values of utility.

Even after identification of the client, the expectations about that role can be confusing. Situations vary depending on whether the relationship is defined from the perspective of the analyst, while others view the client as the dominant player in the relationship. These variations depend on a range of situations: for example, whether the client is new to the job, whether the designation of the client is clear, the client's past experience dealing with a policy issue, organizational constraints, conflict within the organization, and personal and political differences.

These examples indicate that both defining and dealing with clients continue to be very important in the contemporary world of policy analysis. At the same time, the behaviors and role of the client now make up a very diverse sets of practices and experiences. Clients have moved far from the policy analysis relationship of the 1960s, which was limited to a bond between a cabinet secretary and an economist who served as the analyst in the relationship. Both clients and analysts are found in many nicks and crannies around the globe, in both public and private settings, and with very diverse expectations about what will emerge from their role. The relationship between client and analyst continues to be an ever-changing yet fundamental issue.

It is not unusual for policy analysts – especially younger individuals whose personal values and experiences seem to collide with their work assignments – to find themselves in uncomfortable situations with their clients. Sometimes those clients are implicit rather than explicit, but both types make job responsibilities more difficult.

7 Question Two: The World of Practice vs. the Culture of the Academy

Did the move of policy analysis from its origins in the world of practice to its base in the academic world make a difference? If so, what changes accompanied that shift?

Although it soon found a home within the US higher education world, it is useful to remind oneself that this was a field that emerged from the world of practice. It was clear from Wildavsky's original comments about the elements of a school of public policy analysis that he envisioned a somewhat atypical approach to the creation of a faculty for the School and the role of the field's academic home. His vision of a faculty was more like that of a law school than a traditional social science department since it seemed to emphasize the importance of faculty who had practical experience in the field. At the same time, he assumed that they were excited about creating a new academic site for this inchoate field.

Wildavsky's status on the campus (and nationally) was useful to the School's development. Other institutions of higher education that were interested in creating a policy school made regular visits to Berkeley to see what they were doing. As a result, several concepts (like the 48-hour project requirement and realistic analytical projects with clients) became replicated around the country.

Similarly, the range of academic disciplines represented on the Berkeley faculty became a model for others. The Berkeley faculty was drawn mostly from political science and economic disciplines, but also included sociology, law, and public administration. The faculty members who were recruited in the early years were individuals who were already known to the dean and whose personal interests in both teaching and publishing fitted his expectations. Wildavsky seemed to focus on the level of commitment that each person brought to the effort; their point of identification appeared to be to the focus of the school, its goals, and its challenges, rather than abstract elements of the discipline in which they were trained.

Some of the initial faculty were already on the Berkeley faculty in existing programs and departments. A few had been Wildavsky's students and were lured back to the Berkeley campus from other schools. And a few came to the program from practitioner posts in government- or policy-related organizations. While all could meet the university's existing personnel criteria for employment, their interest and commitment in becoming involved in the creation of a new academic field was clearly important. Most of the original faculty members were hired with tenure so a number of issues that reflected now-traditional academic accountability criteria did not show up on the agenda in the School's earliest years.[19]

While the collectivity of the faculty was fairly diverse in terms of field of training, research methodology approach, teaching style, and policy areas, the first group was an all-male, all-white group with degrees from high-status

---

[19] Budget issues began to emerge in higher education during this period and administrative and financial centralization increased. Departments and programs were sometimes encouraged to make joint appointments with another unit. That meant that faculty might be teaching in several departments or schools, violating one of Wildavsky's original criteria for faculty hiring.

universities. This collective group was expected to create the core curriculum because there was no such off-the-shelf curriculum that could be used at that point.

One of the jokes told during the first years of its operation focused on the shared similarity of interests and background among the core faculty. At one point in the early years, some faculty members realized that a high percentage of faculty members were Jewish men and that they could fulfill the requirements for a traditional Jewish minyon (ten men required for prayer). They were interviewing someone for an open position who had an Irish surname and some members of the faculty commented that they were clearly diversifying the selection. However, they learned that the candidate's mother was Jewish – hence, he fit the majority category.

Much of the original curricular development that had been created through group decision-making was handed down from semester to semester. As a result, this may have preempted new faculty members from changing much of the curriculum. The presence of joint masters degrees (e.g. with law, planning, public health, or social work) gave students an opportunity to diversify their programs and include specialization in specific policy areas in their curriculum. This occurred despite Wildavsky's personal interest in a more generic approach.

By the end of the twentieth century, the list of skill areas that were thought to be relevant to an expert policy analyst had become more extensive. Meltsner's dichotomy between technical skills and political skills was relatively simple. The newer group of skills reached beyond those used in the search for the formulation and adoption of new policies and moved into implementation and evaluation stages of the policy process that often included existing policies and programs. Thus, the practice was likely to include the following skills:

- Case study methods
- Cost–benefit analysis
- Ethical analysis
- Evaluation
- Futures analysis
- Historical analysis
- Implementation analysis
- Interviewing
- Legal analysis
- Microeconomics
- Negotiation, mediation
- Operations research
- Organizational analysis
- Political feasibility analysis
- Public speaking

- Small-group facilitation
- Specific program knowledge
- Statistics
- Survey research methods
- Systems analysis (Radin, 2000, pp. 125–126; Radin, 2013a, pp. 164–165).

The expansion of the curricular offering from an MPP degree to both an MPP and a PhD did seem to have some impact on the values underlying the curriculum and structuring the expectations of the required faculty assessment. Tenure was likely to emphasize publication of research in books and academic journals rather than organizational reports of government agencies and interest groups. Although Wildavsky had recommended that the program would not emphasize work in specific policy areas, that did occur. And it is not surprising that theory found its way into the methodological approaches suggested within the curriculum.

While the academic setting for the program seemed to have moved toward a less experimental emphasis, the practitioner world was exactly the opposite in the last quarter of the twentieth century. The expansion of the policy analysis staffs continued across national, state, and local settings, to legislative bodies and legal settings, and became attached to political debates on a number of national policy issues.[20]

7.1 Science vs. Action

Yet these two worlds – that of science and that of action – often move in opposite directions. These differences were illustrated by the US experience in the infamous Hurricane Katrina.[21] What did the research community know that might have helped the decision-makers faced with that horrible disaster? There are at least eight areas of research that might have been used to help answer the questions that arose during that tragedy:

1. The reality of federalism.
2. The role of the military.
3. Institutionalized racism.
4. The role of private sector responsibility.
5. Organizational culture and history.
6. The complexity of the budget process.
7. Reorganization matters.
8. Problems of implementation of new policies and plans.

---

[20] These included welfare policy, health, employment, and environmental issues. In these cases, policy analysts were often at the decision-making table but they were rarely the main players.

[21] This discussion was drawn from Radin, 2013b.

These areas all suggest that relevant insights from public administration, policy, and other political science research areas were not given the opportunity to influence the Katrina decision-making process. Indeed, those involved as decision-makers in that process gave no indication that they were the least bit interested in learning about this body of work. There is little evidence that advice had been sought by those charged with responsibility for decisions. Further, it does not appear that there were individuals poised to provide that kind of advice to those in power. Ironically, those leaders wrapped themselves in arguments for centralization and technical fixes that avoided the political realities that surrounded their positions. This was despite the reality that raw politics overwhelmed so many of the strategies that emerged from the decisions.

7.2 John Gaus

John Gaus, the namesake of the award at which these observations were made, was described thus in the *Dictionary of American Political Scientists*: "Three interrelated themes weave their way through his writings: a rejection of the traditional notion of the separation of politics and administration, the openness of public organizations to their environmental influences, and the responsibility of positive, affirmative government in responding to national crises and emergencies" (Utter and Lockhart, 2002, p. 127).

It was my reading of a rather obscure work by Gaus, "A Study of Research in Public Administration," that gave me the richest perspective on him. This was a report written by Gaus in 1930 for the Advisory Committee on Public Administration of the Social Science Research Council and available only in the original typing (Gaus, 1930, cited in Radin, 2013b).

Writing just before the New Deal, Gaus provided a picture of a society – not simply public organizations – that found itself recovering from World War I, absorbing immigrants, dealing with social and political change, involving the public as well as universities, and seeking to figure out what role government would play in those activities. He described issues that a few years later became a part of President Franklin D. Roosevelt's agenda and contributed directly to the world of the New Deal.

The themes that emerged from Gaus' study of research in public administration seem extremely topical today. He approached these themes not as a skeptic but as someone who was always looking for new responses to new issues. He focused on the reality of constant change as well as the importance of government structure. And he provided significant advice on research. He told us that research occurs at many points and in many forms. It does not occur only in universities. He noted that research and action in administration belongs to many professions, including the law, medicine, engineers, city planners, educators, business, and agriculture. Rarely do we engage in collaborative research.

It is tempting to place the blame for those developments on the demand side – those in positions of authority. But what about the supply side? We can fast forward to 2012 and assess how the policy/public administration research community responded to the Katrina disaster. Three of the top journals in that field were examined to see how they dealt with Hurricane Katrina. One of the journals contained 121 articles that included some discussion of Hurricane Katrina. However, only 21 of those articles had the word "Katrina" in their title. The titles of the other articles included terms such as emergency management, disaster, and crisis but most of them were titled with generic management terms and used Katrina as an example of broader theoretical and generic questions.

Another journal included 22 submissions that dealt with Katrina issues but none of the pieces included the word "Katrina" in their title. Like the other journal, these articles focused on generic and theoretical issues such as networks, contracting, patronage, collaboration, strategies, media, and coalition development. Similarly, the third journal included 21 submissions (19 articles and 2 book reviews) but none of the articles had the word "Katrina" in their title.

This pattern suggests that researchers were not interested in emphasizing the unique aspects of the Katrina disaster, but were focused on broader theoretical issues. It mirrored a pattern in the policy/public administration field in which journals contain relatively few articles dealing with racism and poverty. More importantly, it illustrates the divide between practitioners and researchers. While much of the academic work might be applicable to the situation, it was not conceptualized in a way that was accessible to practitioners. The practitioners were likely to view the emergent research as focused on broader questions that would be of limited interest to them. And it is also likely that the researchers perceived the practitioners as having a narrow view of these intellectually challenging issues. Both of these groups are right, and both are also wrong.

While there were some individuals in both communities who had reached out beyond the traditional divide, the response to Katrina clearly illustrates the limits of those relationships and the failure of both communities to find ways to enrich their understandings by interacting with one another. It is increasingly rare that players in the world of practice find ways to bring their agendas and insights to the academy.

The view of the practitioner/decision-maker that emerges from Gaus' work requires modesty about authority, acceptance of uncertainty, contains multiple actors from multiple sectors, and acknowledges constant change emerging from the external environment. It embraces multiple goals and often conflicting values and expects both optimistic and pessimistic responses from the citizenry. Further, it accepts the limits of technical responses within a political environment as well as the realization that the US skepticism about government power and authority embedded in government structures creates fragmented and diffuse systems.

7.3 Are we Destined to Continue this Pattern?

Will practitioners operate in their independent sphere while researchers focus on abstract and generic issues? Will academics be able to meet the needs of their MPA and MPP students who are entering the world of practice? While the reward structure of both worlds makes it extremely difficult for them to institutionalize shared perspectives, the consequences of those divisions are too important for us to continue as we have over the past several decades.

We are challenged to think about the consequences of an emergency issue like Katrina or COVID-19 by searching for ways that that scholars can try to reach across those divisions. This can be done in several ways.

First, schools and departments can encourage faculty members to spend time within organizations involved in the policymaking and management processes. Wildavsky sought to encourage this through utilizing existing mechanisms (such as sabbaticals and leaves). But is increasingly uncommon today for junior faculty to even think about such an experience.

These opportunities would provide faculty with direct knowledge of decision-making. This might discourage them from working in a narrow research environment.

Second, faculty can seek out opportunities to collaborate with practitioners in research efforts, drawing on suggestions made by Donald Schon years ago (Schon, quoted in Radin, 2013b). As Schon noted, these collaborations not only provide opportunities for faculty to comprehend the world of the practitioner, but also provide the practitioner with opportunities to reflect on their experience, drawing on conceptual frameworks that academics might bring to the exchange.

And, third, schools and departments can redefine the way that they think about their adjunct faculty. Too often adjuncts are seen simply as practitioners who are cheap labor and who fill teaching slots. I am always amazed and heartened at the willingness of such individuals to spend significant time in their teaching role with minimal compensation. But adjuncts can also bring other attributes to the academic setting. Their experience pushes the limits of the textbooks and traditional syllabi to bring new ideas to the academy. They provide essential career counseling to students who desire practitioner careers, not traditional academic pathways. Rarely are the adjuncts rewarded for their contributions.

8 Question Three: Changes in the Environment of Policy Analysis

Did changes in both the internal and external environments of policy analysis make a difference? These could have focused on the effects of constant change, globalization, differentiation between public and private sectors, and organization structure (e.g. networks, shared powers).

As this volume emphasizes, the field of policy analysis and the role of policy analysts have been modified over the life span of the activities that have come to be defined as policy analysis. These modifications have occurred as policy analysts have attempted to respond to quite dramatic changes in the environment that surrounds their efforts. Given the extent of these changes, it sometimes is difficult to identify the vestiges of the original image of a policy analyst. While there continued to be economists found in the US DoD with assignments that focused only on the lowest cost for expenditures in that organization, much more diversity could be found in the profession if its practitioners thought about modifying their work. While it did not take long for modifications to occur in the original expectations, there was a tendency for some participants in the field to hold on to the early descriptions when they were asked to describe their work.

Yet major changes in the profession were found in the last quarter of the twentieth century and the first two decades of the twenty-first century, both in the United States and globally. The post–Cold War environment created space for new relationships and expectations that modified past work. Three areas of change are identified in this discussion that emerged from both the external and internal environments of policy analysis that seem to be particularly relevant and shifted the field from one that was focused internally on the United States to reach beyond America's borders. These involved globalization and constant change and a blurring of the line between public and private sector activities, and reflected different expectations about organization structure (Radin, 2012, chapter 2).

The original policy analysts in the DoD had a relatively easy time mapping their policy environment. They were advising the cabinet secretary and tried to limit their advice to the realities of a hierarchical organization with clear lines of authority. The functions of the DoD appear clear and obvious to the analysts.

While some analysts probably paid attention to the congressional committees that had authority over the agency (and the interests of a range of private sector groups who were likely to receive contracts that emerged from the completed budget), the structure of the PPBS did not really encourage analysts to raise these questions. It was also relevant that these analytic activities emerged originally from a positive economic climate (one that did not start from an assumption of limited resources).

By the time that policy analysis spread to other agencies, the American society was in the midst of a "guns and butter" environment where the cost of the Viet Nam war grew at the same time that the war on poverty received attention. And the congressional committees that had jurisdiction over both sets of programs often moved from authorizing committees (focusing on the specific details of programs) to appropriations committees (wherein committee members highlighted the budget allocations to specific programs). In addition, a number of domestic programs were created that involved implementation by state and local agencies (who lobbied for funds to meet the new expectations). In some program areas (e.g. elementary and secondary education), the policy debate often moved from the question of modifying the federal role to a discussion about how much money should be allocated to the sector.

Each time a program was modified (either expanded or contracted) it was likely that a new group of actors would appear on a map of players within its environment or a different group might leave the analysis. In addition, the results of both presidential and congressional elections would be likely to change the composition of the individuals and groups who influenced the decision-making process.

By the end of the twentieth century there were several changes that had a dramatic impact on the way that policy analysts were expected to define the environment which they dealt with in their work. Globalization of climate issues required analysts to include a range of actors outside the borders of the home country since many issues and problems did not stop at the edge of the interested country.

The slogan "think globally, act locally" called on analysts and their clients to consider the health of the entire planet and to take action in their own communities and cities. Multinational organizations emerged in a number of policy fields that employed policy analysts to help them think through their role and options for change. While they did not affect all policy issues, they became increasingly important in others.[22]

Another change that affected the policy environment involved an increased use of the experience and perspectives of the private sector. The differences

---

[22] These globalization changes merged with increased international interest in policy analysis and stimulated the creation of the *Journal of Comparative Policy Analysis*, now more than twenty years old, and a new focus on publication of non-US articles in other journals.

between public and private goals had been debated in the USA for many years, but the results of that debate had caused the pendulum to move back and forth between the two perspectives (Hirschman, 1982, p. 2). Increased use of contracting-out staff, replacing government officials, was found across the globe. Other private sector experience was used as the model for options and public sector activity, as well as other elements of policy analysis work. Analysts began to understand that the relative importance of different goals varies across regimes and societies, and is often embedded in the assumptions and expectations of the relevant client (Weimer, 2012, p. 4).

The last shift that had an impact on changes involving the environment of policy analysis work was found in the structure of government itself. Over the years it had become clearer that the hierarchical organizational model that supported PPBS (as well as some subsequent techniques) had been replaced in a number of settings by organizational forms that were more complex and produced questions and uncertainties about achievement of policy goals. It also seemed that policy analysts who worked on policy problems that crossed process and substantive lines found themselves with networks as clients (that is, participants who were interested in the policy issues, reached across a range of organizational boundaries, and had different answers to the problem) (Radin, 2019, p. 63).

9 Question Four: Information, Analytic Techniques, and Evidence

Were there changes in the repertoire of analytic techniques used by policy analysts? Where did they come from (e.g. other disciplines, private sector, data sources)? Did the focus on evidence make any difference?

Bardach has noted that policy analysts need information for three principal purposes: First, to assess the nature and extent of the problem; second, to assess the particular features of the specific policy situation; and third, to assess policies that have been thought by some to work effectively in similar situations (Bardach, 2009, p. 83).

Because the early policy analysts were most likely to focus on the creation of new policies, the data they sought was frequently information that documented the need for the policy (conditions that caused the problem within the society or organization) and sometimes provided a general sense of how a proposed policy would operate. By the time analysts were dealing with problems that emerged from existing policies (highlighting the implementation process) they were faced with complex relationships and issues that emerged from existing operations.

At that point, analysts looked to information that was already collected for assistance. In some instances, information that was collected to monitor agencies was the only information that was available but it did not always address the problems that these analysts were addressing. It was not unusual for organizations to collect information at an aggregate level that highlighted the formal accountability relationships in a hierarchical structure. It was not common in many settings to present data that was disaggregated by race, gender, or other specific population categories. And it most often relied on data that was compatible with presentation in a quantitative form rather than qualitative definitions. The type of data sought was conditioned by the analytic techniques chosen by the analyst or the client. These issues are not always obvious, and there may be biases in the data set that reflect issues that may actually skew the findings. In a few instances (for example, the environmental impact statement), analytical techniques were created especially to gather information to meet public sector authority.

9.1 What are the Sources of Information?

Over the years, policy analysts have drawn on many different sources of information. As noted earlier, the choice of tools or analytic method can predetermine the information source. At one point, Bardach suggested that the appropriate techniques for the policy analyst were more like those of a journalist than a social scientist. Others have described the data that is used by policy analysts as information that is "found" rather than manufactured. Martha Feldman described the process as one in which information is found in unexpected places or gathered in unconventional ways (Feldman, 1989, pp. 20–21). Others have relied on visits to organizations and agencies to observe the practices related to the policy problem. Some analysts have found ways of utilizing information produced by social media to illustrate different behaviors.

The practice in the twenty-first century of involving both private sector and public sector institutions in policymaking has led to difficulties when the private sector consid ers information to be of a proprietary nature. Similarly, a federalism structure can make it difficult to collect comparable information from local, provincial, or state sources.

9.2 The Emergence of the Evidence Movement

Around 2010, a new approach to information emerged in the United States and in a number of other countries. In many ways it was a variation on the academic approaches that had already been a part of the policy analysis field. Called the "evidence movement," it was a new way of searching for political neutrality. It was similar to the PPBS in the 1960s in some ways and reflected a belief in the potential of analytic skills and the ability to devise a rational framework that would produce neutral data.

PPBS was followed by other efforts that rested on several assumptions: that information is available, that information is neutral, that it is possible to define cause–effect relationships, and that almost all activities can be measured and quantified. Many analysts thought that this information could serve as the tool for defining the policy problem, as the way of choosing between options, and as the way of making a recommendation (Putansu, 2020, chapter 2).

As discussed, the initial activities that emerged from the first policy analysts in the US DoD were crafted around the PPBS analytical technique. The decisions that emerged from the use of this technique involved allocation of budget resources at the departmental level for staff, equipment, and research activities and authorities that had been present in the separate entities within the department (e.g. the Army, Air Force, Navy, Marines). In addition, much of that authority was actually claimed by congressional players, not executive-level officials.

Many of the economists who were involved in these initial analytical activities were comfortable with the demands implicit in this analytical process and valued the results of their work. Indeed, the decision by President Johnson to apply the technique to the entire federal government suggests that optimistic view. Moving out of the defense world did, however, raise a number of questions about the appropriateness of the PPBS technique in different settings.

Wildavsky's critique and analysis of the limits of PPBS brought a series of insights from the political science literature to the developing policy analysis field. At the very least, it provided a way for analysts to consider options in the decision process, acknowledging that decision-makers were facing a complex set of policy approaches. The use of benefit–cost analysis seemed to offer a way for analysts to identify impacts of potential alternatives focusing on constraints such as time and risk. The first step in the process was to consider impacts of the alternative under review and determine whether they were costs or benefits for various players (Weimer and Vining, 1989, p. 265).

While both PPBS and benefit–cost analysis continued to bring an economist's perspective to the desk of a decision-maker in a hierarchical organization, the traditional economists' view did not fit easily with policy questions that emerged from the assessment of implementation of existing policies. At this point, policy analysts found resources in the sociology discipline and began to draw on approaches that emerged from this traditional social science field that rested on the norms of experimentation and value-free approaches.

In many cases, the implementation of existing programs became the focus of the policy analyst's portfolio and analysts sought a way to use data collected for management and oversight purposes as the basis for new options. In that sense, the analysts were confronting the same issue that public administration people had faced for many years: Is there is a clear dichotomy between politics and administration? Both scholars and practitioners were trying to identify a set of activities that seemed to transcend partisan politics. Were they clear, neutral, and lasting? Many data systems were built to provide information that could justify the continuation of an existing program or policy. Yet it was often difficult to disentangle motives for data collection, and implementators often found themselves joining economists and using arguments based on numbers to make their case.

By the 1980s, the naïve perspective was confronted by several extremely interesting writers who sought new ways to think about policy information. Lindblom and Cohen's 1989 volume, *Useable Knowledge: Social Science and Social Problem Solving*, contrasted the approach to information from academic social science with what they called ordinary knowledge – information from common-sense speculation and analysis.

Carol Weiss published "Ideology, Interests, and Information: The Basis of Policy Positions" (in Callahan and Jennings, 1983). She wrote: "Observers who expect the subcategory of information that is social science research to have immediate and independent power in the process, and who bitterly complain about the intrusion of 'politics' ... into the use of research, implicitly hold a distorted view of how decisions are made" (Weiss, 1983, pp. 221–222; Putansu, 2020, chapter 2).

Giandomenico Majone was one of the more critical observers of these efforts. He viewed the analyst as one who pays the role of participant and mediator rather than objective scientist (Majone, 1989). Evidence for him was much closer to the process used in legal reasoning: it was information that is used to make a case.

But the faith in information was particularly important in the emergent evaluation field. Alice Rivlin described the federal government in the late 1960s. She commented that "Both advocates and evaluators were naïve by today's standards. We all thought that simple interventions could change lives and evaluation would show clear results quickly. It gradually dawned on all of us that progress was going to be more complicated" (Rivlin, 2014). In addition, policy analysts in the early days of the field were likely to have resources that allowed them to actually collect data that could be used specifically for the analytical work the staff could undertake. Often those resources quickly became limited and did not provide the type of information that the staff members had envisioned (Radin, 2016b).

The use of the term "evidence" in this setting was very different from the way that "evidence" is defined in the legal system. In that system the advocate determines the best solution to a client's problem and the term "evidence" refers to anything that can be used to justify that solution. Evidence thus can be used to prove that something exists or proof that other perspectives are not true.

Despite the legal profession's claim to the concept of evidence, the US Congress enacted legislation in 2016 creating the Commission on Evidence-Based Policymaking. The Commission was given a year "to study and develop a strategy for strengthening government's evidence building and policymaking efforts" (Report of the Commission on Evidence-Based Policymaking, 2017, p. 1). It highlighted its goal: "rigorous evidence is created efficiently, as a routine part of government operations, and used to construct effective public policy." The Commission argued that "the greater use of existing data is now possible in conjunction with stronger privacy and legal protections, as well as increased transparency and accountability." (Ibid)

According to the Commission, this effort grew out of the historical view in the United States recognizing the importance of the role of the Census Bureau to provide information for governance and, as well, the data provided in units within the government to develop policy information. The report defined "evidence" as information produced by "statistical activities" with a "statistical purpose" and envisioned a strong role for the centralized budget office – US Office of Management and Budget.

In addition to the role defined by the Report of the Commission on Evidence-Based Policymaking, the "evidence movement" has moved in several other directions. A group of social policy experts (called the Friends of Evidence) has attempted to focus on defining what constitutes useful and useable evidence, not that all information is appropriate. Others have linked the movement to a single research methodology: randomized controlled trials. Still others have argued that traditional social science (such as program evaluation) can be combined with data science (big data, data mining, predictive modeling, and artificial intelligence).

The expectations surrounding the "evidence movement" do not always jibe with the situations that policy analysts find themselves in. There is a range of constraints that have limited their application. These problem areas include:

- Multiple goals in many public policy problems and programs
- Issues that seem to be attached to implementation from the past
- Anticipating uncertainty and change
- Responding to cultural norms
- Dealing with an advocacy role (especially when the program was being attacked)
- The limits of formal data systems

- Limits of research-produced data
- Availability of "big data" for analysts
- Ability to use information to facilitate bargaining and tradeoffs (Radin, 2019, p. 95).

10 Question Five: Values

What values structured the analytic process (e.g. efficiency, equity, effectiveness)? Were values built into some policy issues and policy cultures? Was the search for theory related to tendencies to one size fits all situations?

The original focus on PPBS in the early days of policy analysis seemed to emphasize efficiency values above all possible goals of the new profession. Given the prominence of economists at that time, that emphasis was not surprising. When benefit–cost analysis became a favorite technique, effectiveness goals were added to the efficiency objectives built into the analytical process.

It took some time for policy analysts to also focus on equity (Okun, 2015) as the third "E," although the years of the Johnson administration established a number of programs that had clear program goals that sought to redistribute power and a range of resources across the society. Theodore Lowi developed a typology in 1972 that was used by some policy analysts to differentiate between programs that had diverse types of coercion, policy types, and political types (Lowi, 1972, p. 300).

10.1 Relying on the Budget

The ascendency of the budget process in US government decision-making during the last quarter of the twentieth century tended to emphasize issues related to measurement of efficiency of resources rather than the programmatic substance of the policy being developed (which dealt with effectiveness and equity issues). This also opened the door to values and techniques that had been traditionally a part of private sector decision-making.

Table 3 Lowi Typology of Policies

Distributive policy	Constituent policy
Regulative policy	Redistributive policy

Drawn from Lowi, 1972

10.2 Policy Cultures

Policy analysts who developed specializations in specific policy areas also became aware of values that were implicit in the cultures of these policy fields. For example, programs dealing with elementary and secondary education could not deal only with their direct client (the student in school) because the children were young and required the involvement of their parents, who were their advocates. That principle applied to a number of programs wherein the direct client was not able to agree to specific treatments and programs.

The social and economic status of the service provider could also affect the way that a policy was treated in political debate. Health programs seem always to be balancing a number of competing requirements dealing with provision of care to those who need it, the cost of the service, and the willingness of health providers (who have high status in the society) to participate. Thus, when physicians appear at policy or budget hearings they often receive an unusually deferential response from the members of Congress (Weimer, 2012).

A new policy analyst who has not been attuned to the unique attributes of a policy culture through previous work in that policy area is rarely exposed to this type of information in their academic training. They may be more influenced by theoretical frameworks that tend to support "one size fits all" approaches that have emerged from generic theoretical approaches or past arguments that are limited by specialized theories that depend on the biases of information that is available or collected for other purposes.

Policy analysts may be becoming more sensitive to the diverse cultures of different settings when they focus on comparative policy analysis across the globe, but there is still a tendency for analysts to minimize those differences. Cultures are difficult to label or to describe, but they can make a great difference in understanding the context and reactions to both options and decision-making processes (see Uhr and Mackay, 1996; also Scott and Baehler, 2010; Colebatch, 2006).

It is clear that there is not a single model that one can use to describe the activities and approaches of an individual who self-defines as a policy analyst. The following questionnaire has been developed to help readers place themselves in the field. There is no "right" answer to the questions that follow, but the patterns and answers that emerge from this list of questions might help us identify a range of individuals who have a legitimate claim on this important role.

11 Conclusion

As this analysis has indicated, it is clear that searching for a clear definition of the field of policy analysis is a difficult – perhaps impossible – effort.

Policy analysis is a field that is full of contradictory approaches, assumptions, and arguments. Diversity is a reality that is built into its history as well as its present. There is no agreed-upon definition of what to do or what criteria to use to evaluate the work produced under the rubric of policy analysis.

At the same time, the development of the field over more than half a century has produced a rich array of concepts that are located around the globe, are found in many different institutions of higher education, and are the main subject of a number of journals and other publications. It has spawned national and international organizations which generate debate about a wide range of possibilities.

There were times in its history that policy analysts brought a belief in possibility and change to the society. But there were other times when they were the messengers of gloom and doom. This analysis has attempted to acknowledge the legitimacy of this variety of approaches. This volume has emphasized several dichotomies that flow from the literature. They include the analyst vs. the client, research vs. practice, efficiency vs. equity, and advocates vs. analysts. There is not a single definition of the term "policy analyst" that would be agreed to by all those who define themselves under that rubric.

As it developed, the field itself experienced growing pains, and definitions of success in the practice of policy analysis were not always obvious or agreed upon. Several questions were difficult to answer. Was success the ability to convince the client/decision-maker to adopt your recommendation? Was an analyst successful when he or she helped the client understand the complexity and dimensions of a policy choice? Was the analyst successful when the work that was performed was publishable and approved by one's peers within the profession? The norms behind each of these questions suggested that policy analysis is a field that embraced the values of science, neutrality, and research at the same time that it also embraced pragmatic values of utility. Its challenge is to live with that tension.

12 Section Three: The Questionnaire. What Does It Mean to Be a Policy Analyst?

I hope that the reader of this volume completes reading this with a belief that there is not a single model that one can use to describe the activities and approaches of an individual who self-defines as a policy analyst. The following questionnaire has been developed to help readers place themselves in the field through their descriptions and responses to a range of questions. There is no "right" answer to the questions that follow; rather, the patterns and answers that emerge from this list of questions might help us identify a range of individuals who have a legitimate claim on this important role.

The questionnaire that is included in this conclusion provides an opportunity for the readers of this work to describe their personal experiences and definition of their work. This author would be pleased to hear from readers and find a way to name and characterize the different experiences of those who march under the policy analysis banner.

Please complete this questionnaire

1. Where are you in terms of your career development?

   At the beginning of career
   Mid-career
   Close to retirement

2. Job Title

3. What is your academic background?

   Economics
   Political Science
   Sociology
   Planning
   Business
   Other

4. How would you describe your approach to the field?

   A technician
   An advocate
   A politician
   A facilitator
   A researcher
   A practitioner
   An evaluator
   An analyst
   An economist
   A manager
   Other

5. Have you specialized in a policy area?

   No
   Yes
                  What area?
                  Familiarity with specific problem

6. Have you specialized in a level of government or sector?

   National
   State, regional, or local
   Nonprofit
   For-profit
   Other

7. What is your major goal as a policy analyst?

   Job promotion
   Publication
   Influence change
   Other
   Please answer the following questions about a relatively recent policy analysis assignment that you have been involved with:

1. What was the topic of the assignment?

2. How did it get to you?

   Self-generated
   Came from my supervisor
   Predictable requirement
   Came from crisis situation
   Other

3. In what order did you make the following choices or take action? Rank as *essential*, *useful*, or *not required* in the situation you are using as the example.

Rank 1: Essential
Rank 2: Useful
Rank 3: Not required

_____

Decide whether there is a client

Rank 1 or 2
If 1 or 2: single person or multiple perspectives
Rank 3: why?

Discussion of mode of communication with client, staff, others

For schedule: Rank
For options: Rank
For drafts: Rank
For approval: Rank

Define the policy problem

Rank
Who involved: Client, staff, others

Decide on methodology and analytical technique

Rank
Who involved: Client, staff, others

Decide on source of data

Rank
Who involved: Client, staff, others

Identify limitations of data

Rank
Who involved: Client, staff, others

Decide on theory and working hypotheses

Rank
Who involved: Client, staff, others

Identify areas of expected controversy

Rank
Players in controversy:
On what:

4. What was result of the work?

Met expectations
Led to other assignments
Never finished
Other

5. If you could start over on the project, what would you do differently?

References

Bardach, Eugene, 2009, *A Practical Guide for Policy Analysis: The Eightfold Path to More Effective Problem Solving, Third Edition* (Washington, DC: CQ Press).

Bardach, Eugene and Eric M. Patashnik, 2016, *A Practical Guide for Policy Analysis: The Eightfold Path to More Effective Problem Solving, Fifth Edition* (Los Angeles: Sage CQ Press).

Colebatch, H. K. editor, 2006, *The Work of Policy: An International Survey* (Lanham: Lexington Books).

Commission on Evidence-Based Policeymaking, 2017, Report of the Commission on Evidence-Based Policymaking: "The Promise of Evidence-Based Policymaking" (Washington, DC).

Douglas, Mary and Aaron Wildavsky, 1983, *Risk and Culture* (Berkeley: University of California Press).

Dror, Yehezkel, 1971, *Ventures in Policy Sciences* (New York: Elsevier).

Feldman, Martha, 1989, *Order Without Design: Information Production and Policy Making* (Stanford: Stanford University Press).

Geva-May, Iris, 1997, *An Operational Approach to Policy Analysis: The Craft: Prescriptions for Better Analysis* (Boston: Klumer Academic Publishers).

     editor, 2005, *Thinking Like a Policy Analyst: Policy Analysis as a Clinical Profession* (Chennai: Palgrave MacMillan).

Goldhamer, Herbert, 1978, *The Adviser* (New York: Elsevier).

Hird, John A., editor, 2018, *Policy Analysis in the United States* (Bristol: Policy Press).

Hirschman, Albert O. 1982, *Shifting Involvements: Private Interest and Public Action* (Princeton: Princeton University Press).

Hogwood, Brian W. and Lewis A. Gunn, 1984, *Policy Analysis for the Real World* (Oxford: Oxford University Press).

Laswell, Harold D., 1970, "The Emerging Conception of the Policy Sciences," *Policy Sciences*, Vol. 1, *No. 1*, Spring, 3–30.

Lindblom, C. E. and D. K. Cohen, 1989, *Useable Knowledge: Social Science and Social Problem Solving* (New Haven: Yale University Press).

Lowi, Theodore J., 1972, "Four Systems of Policy, Politics and Choice," *Public Administration Review*, Vol. 32, *No. 4* (July-Aug), 298–310.

Majone, Giandomenico, 1989. *Evidence, Argument, and Persuasion in the Policy Process* (New Haven: Yale University Press).

Meltsner, Arnold J., 1976, *Policy Analysts in the Bureaucracy* (Berkeley: University of California Press).

1986, "The Seven Deadly Sins of Policy Analysis," *Science Communication*, 7:367. DOI: 10.1177/107554708600700402.

1990, *Rules for Rulers: The Politics of Advice* (Philadelphia: Temple University Press).

Nienaber Clarke, Jeanne and Helen Ingram, 2010, "A Founder: Aaron Wildavsky and the Study of Public Policy," *Policy Studies Journal*, 11 Sept., 565–579.

Okun, Arthur M., 2015, *Equality and Efficiency: The Big Tradeoff* (A Brookings Classic) (Washington, DC: Brookings).

Putansu, Steven, 2020, *Politics and Policy Knowledge in Federal Education: Confronting the Evidence-Based Proverb* (Switzerland: Palgrave Macmillan).

Radin, Beryl A., 1997, "Presidential Address: The Evolution of the Policy Analysis Field: From Conversation to Conversations?" *Journal of Policy Analysis and Management*, 16:2, 204–218.

2000, *Beyond Machiavelli: Policy Analysis Comes of Age* (Washington, DC: Georgetown University Press).

2012, *Federal Management Reform in a World of Contradictions* (Washington, DC: Georgetown University Press).

2013a, *Beyond Machiavelli: Policy Analysis Reaches Midlife, Second Edition* (Washington, DC: Georgetown University Press).

2013b, "Reclaiming Our Past: Linking Theory and Practice," The 2012 John Gaus Lecture, PS, January 2013, 1–7.

2013c, "Policy Analysis Reaches Mid Life," *Central European Journal of Public Policy*, Vol. 7, No. 1 (June), 8–27.

2016a, "Policy Analysis and Advising Decisionmakers: Don't Forget the Decisionmaker/Client," *Journal of Comparative Policy Analysis: Research and Practice*, Vol. 18, Number 3 (June), 290–301.

2016b, Book Review: "Neutral Information, Evidence, Politics, and Public Administration", review of Ron Hoskins and Greg Margolis, Show Me the Evidence: Obama's Fight for Rigor and Results in Social Policy, and Jim Nussle and Peter Orszag, Moneyball for Government," in *Public Administration Review*, January/February 2016, Vol. 76, Issue 1, 188–192.

2017, "Reflections on a Half Century of Policy Analysis," in Marlene Brans, Iris Geva-May and Michael Howlett, editors, *Routledge Handbook of Comparative Policy* (Bristol: Routledge)

2018, "The Evolution of the Policy Analysis Profession in the United States," in John Hird, editor, *Policy Analysis in the United States* (Bristol: Policy Press, 85–99).

2019, *Policy Analysis in the Twenty-First Century: Complexity, Conflict and Cases* (New York: Routledge).

Radin, Beryl A. and David L. Weimer, 2018, "Compared to What? The Multiple Meanings of Comparative Policy Analysis," *Journal of Comparative Policy Analysis*, Vol. 20, Issue 1, 56–71. https://doi.org/10.1080/13876988.2017.1414475.

Rivlin, Alice, 2014, "Keynote Speech to Friends of Evidence," November 13, 2014

Scott, Claudia and Karen Baehler, 2010, *Adding Value to Policy Analysis and Advice* (Sydney: University of New South Wales Press).

Stone, Deborah, 1997, *Policy Paradox: The Art of Political Decision Making* (New York: W. W. Norton and Co. Jr.).

Uhr, John and Keith Mackay, editors, 1996, *Evaluating Policy Advice: Learning from Commonwealth Experience* (Canberra: The Australian National University and Commonwealth Department of Finance).

Utter, Glenn H. , and Charles Lockhart, editors, 2002, *American Political Scientists: A Dictionary* (New York: ABC-CLIO).

Vining, Aidan R. and David L. Weimer, 2010, "The Foundations of Public Administration, Policy Analysis," *Public Administration Review, ASPA Special Publication*.

Weimer, D. J., 2012, "The Universal and the Particular in Policy Analysis and Training," *Journal of Comparative Policy Analysis*, Vol. 14, Issue 1, 4.

Weimer, David L. and Aidan R. Vining, 1987/1989/1999, *Policy Analysis Concepts and Practice (First Edition, Second Edition, Third Edition)* (Englewood Cliffs: Prentice Hall).

Weiss, Carol H. 1983. "Ideology, Interests, and Information: The Basis of Policy Positions." In D. Callahan and B. Jennings, editors, *Ethics, the Social Sciences, and Policy Analysis* (New York: Plenum Press).

editor, 1992, *Organizations for Policy Analysis: Helping Government Think* (Newbury Park: Sage Publications).

Wildavsky, Aaron, 1964, *The Politics of the Budgetary Process* (Boston: Little Brown).

1969, "The Road to PPB: The Stages of Budget Reform," *Public Administration Review*, 29, 189–202.

1979, *Speaking Truth to Power: The Art and Craft of Policy Analysis*, original edition (Boston: Little, Brown and Company).

1987, *Speaking Truth to Power: The Art and Craft of Policy Analysis*, with a new introduction by the author (New Brunswick: Transaction Books).

About the Author

Beryl A. Radin is an author, researcher and academic. She has taught at Georgetown University, American University, SUNY Albany, and the University of Southern California. She calls herself a pracademic. An elected member of the National Academy of Public Administration, she was the Managing Editor of the *Journal of Public Administration Research and Theory* from 2000 to 2005. She created and served as the editor of the Georgetown University Press book series Public Management and Change. Her government service included two years as a Special Advisor to the Assistant Secretary for Management and Budget of the US Department of Health and Human Services and other agencies and a range of consultancies.

Professor Radin has written more than a dozen books and many articles on public policy and public management issues. Much of her work has focused on policy analysis, intergovernmental relationships, and federal management change. Her recent work has focused on comparative policy analysis. Her most recent books are *Policy Analysis in the Twenty-First Century: Complexity, Conflict and Cases*, as well as the second edition of her book on the history of the policy analysis. Her work has involved experience in Australia, India, Israel, Azerbaijan, Hong Kong, and Canada.

Public Policy

M. Ramesh
National University of Singapore (NUS)

M. Ramesh is UNESCO Chair on Social Policy Design at the Lee Kuan Yew School of Public Policy, NUS. His research focuses on governance and social policy in East and Southeast Asia, in addition to public policy institutions and processes. He has published extensively in reputed international journals. He is co-editor of *Policy and Society* and *Policy Design and Practice*.

Michael Howlett
Simon Fraser University, British Colombia

Michael Howlett is Burnaby Mountain Professor and Canada Research Chair (Tier 1) in the Department of Political Science, Simon Fraser University. He specialises in public policy analysis, and resource and environmental policy. He is currently editor-in-chief of *Policy Sciences* and co-editor of the *Journal of Comparative Policy Analysis; Policy and Society* and *Policy Design and Practice*.

Xun Wu
Hong Kong University of Science and Technology

Xun Wu is Professor and Head of the Division of Public Policy at the Hong Kong University of Science and Technology. He is a policy scientist whose research interests include policy innovations, water resource management and health policy reform. He has been involved extensively in consultancy and executive education, his work involving consultations for the World Bank and UNEP.

Judith Clifton
University of Cantabria

Judith Clifton is Professor of Economics at the University of Cantabria, Spain. She has published in leading policy journals and is editor-in-chief of the *Journal of Economic Policy Reform*. Most recently, her research enquires how emerging technologies can transform public administration, a forward-looking cutting-edge project which received €3.5 million funding from the Horizon2020 programme.

Eduardo Araral
National University of Singapore (NUS)

Eduardo Araral is widely published in various journals and books and has presented in forty conferences. He is currently Co-Director of the Institute of Water Policy at the Lee Kuan Yew School of Public Policy, NUS and is a member of the editorial board of *Journal of Public Administration Research and Theory* and the board of the Public Management Research Association.

About the series

Elements in Public Policy is a concise and authoritative collection of assessments of the state of the art and future research directions in public policy research, as well as substantive new research on key topics. Edited by leading scholars in the field, the series is an ideal medium for reflecting on and advancing the understanding of critical issues in the public sphere. Collectively, it provides a forum for broad and diverse coverage of all major topics in the field while integrating different disciplinary and methodological approaches.

Cambridge Elements ≡

Public Policy

Elements in the series

A full series listing is available at: www.cambridge.org/EPPO